FLASHBACKS NO. 16

The Flashback series is sponsored by the
European Ethnological Research Centre,
of Scotland,
Edinburgh EH1 1JF.

Editor: Alexander Fenton

PEAT FIRE MEMORIES

LIFE IN LEWIS IN THE EARLY TWENTIETH CENTURY

Kenneth Macdonald

TUCKWELL PRESS
in association with

THE EUROPEAN ETHNOLOGICAL RESEARCH CENTRE

NM|S
The National Museums of Scotland

First published in Great Britain in 2003 by
Tuckwell Press
The Mill House
Phantassie
East Linton
East Lothian, Scotland

ISBN 1 86232 222 8

Grateful acknowledgement for financial support is made to
Kenneth Macdonald's daughter, Mrs Margaret Murphy,
Canada; to the Sandwick North Street Grazings Committee,
Lewis; and to the Scotland Inheritance Fund

British Library Cataloguing in Publication Data
A catalogue record for this book is available
on request from the British Library

Typeset by Hewer Text Ltd, Edinburgh
Printed and bound by
The Cromwell Press Ltd.

CONTENTS

Kenneth Macdonald, Gaelic newsreader

KENNETH MACDONALD
(1891–1957)

Kenneth Macdonald was a man deeply rooted in the life of his native village of Sandwick, Isle of Lewis. As a teacher, he was kind, sympathetic and exceptionally popular with his pupils at the Nicolson Institute in Stornoway, but his interest in the ordinary folk was what motivated his whole life.

He was intensely involved with all aspects of the community: as Councillor and member of the local Trust, as a Justice of the Peace helping people with official papers, as the prime mover in the establishment of the Co-operative movement in Stornoway; and he was regarded as one of the pioneers of socialism in the Isles at a time when leftist leanings were equated with Bolshevism.

Along with other volunteers, he organised the building of a village hall where social activities such as badminton, debating club, drama club, and concerts could take place. There was a special weekly night for the under-fourteens. Also, he held volunteer continuation classes in Gaelic, English and Mathematics.

Upon moving to Glasgow in 1939, he continued political involvement as election agent for Kelvingrove Labour Party, and socially with the Highland community as treasurer of the Lewis and Harris Association. He quickly rose to the position of Head Teacher (Principal) and was the first to organise and take groups of schoolchildren to Europe.

The embodiment of his feelings for the warm and close-knit Highland way of life prompted his poetry and plays in Gaelic, some of which were broadcast on the BBC, where he was also a Gaelic newsreader. A collection of his poems was published as *Carragh na Cuimhne* in 1991.

This collection of stories gives a glimpse into what life was like as he grew up—and what has irrevocably been lost through the march of progress.

Some of the material in this book first appeared in *Chambers' Journal*

I

THE BLACK HOUSE

There is an old Gaelic proverb which says, 'Tha isean fhein geal leis an fhitheach', meaning 'The raven sees its own fledgling white'. That is how many of us belonging to the older generation who had experience of the black house feel about it. It was pure white in their eyes, the whiteness that was an indication of all that was pure and good. And I am afraid that all the modern conveniences of the white house, its electric light and piped water, will not compensate for what was lost with the disappearance of the black house.

Far more than a mere house disappeared; with it went the traditions of many centuries; a way of life disappeared, a way that had much that was worth preserving. Like many other isles folk who had a foot in the old and the new, the black and the white, I personally mourn its disappearance, and I am not at all sure that the generations which follow in the new house are as happy and contented as their forebears were in the old.

Most people have only seen the black house from the outside, or perhaps an artist's impression of it, usually on a bleak hillside or a lonely glen. In those days there was no housing problem in the isles and the population was much larger than it is today. Today with a lesser population there is a big housing shortage. Why the paradox? The islesman answers it very simply—law and order reached the isles and a way of life was imposed on them that they did not understand. But let me give you an impression of the black house and the building of it.

The materials, stones, earth and turf for the walls, were all on the site. All that was needed was the permission of the village folk to build on the common pasture, and this was given quite readily if you were resident in the village. Not only that, but they all turned out to give a hand with the building. Indeed there were no delays anywhere, and the house was ready in a few days.

There was a reason for the great hurry. No application was made to the local authority for permission or to the Dean of Guild for approval. Even the factor was not consulted, for experience had taught them that, now law and order had reached the isles, refusal was taken for granted. And so it will be understood that to ask for the factor's consent was looking for trouble. Indeed, the main object was to present the factor with a 'fait accompli' before any of his hirelings discovered what had happened. Most Highland factors were tyrants, and their very appearance in any of the villages was associated only with evictions and everything that was evil. Hence the aside of a local woman as the funeral of the factor passed, 'Never has the factor passed through the village as quietly as he did today'.

The walls of the black house consisted of two drystone dykes built about five feet apart and filled in between with trampled earth. The walls tapered as they approached the required height but were still about a yard wide at the top. There were no levels or plumb lines and in general measurements were by eye. The corners were not squared but rounded off so that the plan looked as much like an oval as an oblong.

The biggest difficulty in the isles was the lack of timber as there were no trees to speak of, although there are many indications in the peat moss that they were heavily wooded once upon a time. The writer has seen decayed trunks of trees as thick as a man's body and hazel nuts buried in about six feet of moss. Wood, therefore, was valuable in those days and perhaps the natives could be excused when they gave thanks to God in their prayers for the wrecks which took place around their shores.

The couples for the roof of the black house were usually old cabers or driftwood from the shore. To secure these together, odd pieces were laid on lengthways. Nails were a much later innovation, so the odd pieces were tied on with ropes of straw or heather. There was, of course, no sarking (the boarding on which slates are laid), but slabs of turf about two feet square and two to three inches thick were laid on from the eaves upward in the same manner as tiles or slates are put on a modern house.

The roof was now ready for its covering of thatch, which was usually of straw, although rushes, heather, iris, or bracken were occasionally used. In the old days, when all threshing was done by the flail, not a grain of seed was left on the stalks. Further, the straw remained in its position in the sheaf, all running the same way. This gave a tidy, clean watertight thatch. But with the introduction of the barn threshing mill, the straw was all mixed together and many seeds were left on the straw, with the result that a lovely crop of green oats grew through the top before the summer was out. It was most unsightly but the crofter preferred to leave it because if he disturbed the thatch trying to get it out, the result was more leaky patches than he had before. The lesser of two evils was to leave it alone. It then became the focal point of visiting photographers from the south, who wondered in their ignorance why the 'lazy' people did not cut it down and leave the place nice and tidy. The cruder it looked, the better for the photographer, and neat, tidy cottages would be passed by unnoticed.

Two sticks protruded through the thatch at each end of the house. They served as belaying pins to secure ropes which were passed over the house. The ropes were at intervals of about one foot all along the length of the house and over the ridge to the opposite side. A weight called an 'anchor' was attached to each rope and rested on the thatch about a foot above the eaves. In the old days all the ropes were made of straw or heather but about eighty years ago a local merchant, Charles Morrison, imported rolls of coir rope from the south, and from then onwards it was always this type that was used. And those who still use it today probably do not know why it is called *Sioman Thearlaich*, or Charlie's rope.

After the thatching was complete and the anchors were all set in a line along the front and back, the eaves were trimmed with the sheep shears. The type of house which I am describing really had no eaves. You see, the walls were at least a yard thick on the top and the couples rested on the inner side of the wall, leaving a path right round the house on top of the wall. A rich crop of green grass grew on this path, which was a great attraction for the sheep. They could always be seen there and were often tempted to climb on to the actual thatch to have a mouthful of the sweet green oats which grew further up. It can be understood what great damage this did to the roof. Hens too were attracted by the odd grain of oats which was to be found on the top. A hen needed only five minutes scraping in the thatch to make the whole work useless. Fortunate was the crofter who possessed an old net or a bit of an old trawl to spread over the roof when he was finished thatching. How often could be heard the remark, 'Run, dear, and see if the hens are on the thatch'. And if they were, there was no quarter!

In a few days' time the house was completed as far as the outside was concerned. Next, the inside had to be tackled. Usually there were three rooms, the *culaist* or bedroom, the kitchen, and the byre at the lower end where the cattle were kept. These rooms were separated by a partition of stones and clay. The *culaist* or bedroom was long enough to hold three beds along the wall. The beds were, as a rule, boxed in and had a canopy or roof of their own, as it was not uncommon in very wet weather to have a drip on the bed. A friend of my own told me he had often seen his parents with an umbrella over them in bed!

After a few coats of thatch, the average black house was as watertight as a bottle, but in many cases it was customary to strip the thatch off each year and use the well-sooted straw as manure for the potatoes. This meant, of course, that the house never had more than one coat of thatch. That house was always leaky and conditions inside, in spite of a roaring peat fire, were often very uncomfortable. There was a drip here and there all over the room and it was a case of adjusting oneself between two drips and hoping that spot would keep dry. These trials were taken with good humour, one old bodach commenting to his neighbour that his house was like a watchmaker's shop last night with a tick, tock, in every corner of the room. We can also understand old Domhnull Mor's plight, when after trying hard to adjust himself between two drips, but without success, he got up and went outside commenting, 'It is far better outside than in; at least you can get it clean outside'. Domhnull was right, for every drop that fell left its black sooty mark wherever it struck.

Floors were of clay, and it was customary after laying them to invite the boys of the village to hold a few dances there in order to tramp it down. All floors as a rule sloped towards the cattle end. This was to make sure that no 'liquids' would seep through to the other rooms from the byre. In the main, floors were damp and it was not uncommon to have water oozing through the floor. In fact, I knew of one house which must have had a spring underneath as water was always coming up through the floor. A small hole was scooped in the floor and emptied each time it got full. It was common to spread all the ashes from the hearth on to the floor in order to dry up all the damp spots.

There was only one fire in the house and that was in the kitchen or middle room. The fire was in the middle of the floor, and the smoke found its way as best it could through the thatch. Some houses had a hole in the thatch immediately above the fire. An old bottomless zinc pail served as a chimneycan on top of the thatch.

The hearth was raised to the desired height by adding an extra layer of stones and clay. If one was available, an old cartwheel iron tyre was laid flat on the floor and the inner space filled in with stones and clay. There was a certain kind of very heavy deep-blue clay which was always used for the hearth as it had strong heat-resisting qualities. In my own district it would only be found at low water mark on the shore.

A chain dangled from the spar over the fire. Pots were all of the three-legged variety and all the cooking was done with the pot, the girdle and the brander. Cooking had its difficulties. Light cobwebs of soot continually floated around in the warm air and a heavy coating of it lay on the chain over the fire. All the pots had lids which had to be on when anything was cooking. Sometimes it was even taking a chance to have a peep into the pot when a meal was being prepared. And many a good pot of porridge was ruined while the cautious wife raised the lid and gave the pot a stir with the spurtle. At that very moment a lump of soot would come tumbling down and the meal was ruined. Even with its sooty taste it was often used, for the emptying barrel or meal cist told a tale of harder times to come.

The fire in the middle of the floor had advantages nevertheless. The housewife could get right round it with ease and the chain could swing well out clear of the fire when she was putting on or taking off a pot. This swinging out of the chain was put to use by the young lads of the ceilidh house. Everybody sat round the fire, and when all the chairs and stools were occupied, peats were taken from under the kitchen bed. A latecomer, when about to sit down on his stool of peats, would be suddenly pushed from behind over the fire. The only way he could save himself was by grasping the sooty chain in both hands. When the lads got him in this position he would be kept swinging from side to side until he got a chance to let go without falling into the fire.

The main door entrance was always in the byre end immediately behind the partition separating it from the kitchen. Animals and humans all entered by this door, the animals turning right for the stalls and the humans left for the kitchen. The cattle were tethered to a post attached to the wall of the byre and could turn round and face the opposite way. No manure was removed, but the droppings were spread out daily and a clean bed of turf or straw laid out for the animal. By springtime the accumulated manure was so high that the animal's back was actually touching the roof or thatch. Each spring the far end of the byre was removed to make access for the cart, when the year's accumulation was carted to the croft and the cattle were taken back to terra firma again.

Hens lived in the same apartment as the cattle. They entered through a hole left in the thatch at the far end of the byre and perched on a long spar which ran from side to side of the byre. Old creels or any old boxes served as nesting boxes along the top of the walk. Hens need the warmth in the winter, and the temperature was kept up to normal by the warm breath of the animals and by the smoke which permeated from the kitchen fire. The old folk believed that the hens laid better under these conditions than under the new.

That is a picture of the black house, and I can assure you, with all its lack of hygiene according to modern standards, it was a very happy and contented home.

2

Canvas Town

Many people in the village of Sandwick today would not recognise their village by the name of Canvas Town. Those who knew it as such were scattered far and wide, and little or nothing is generally known of this seafaring community as it was. Well before the turn of the century, this village had established a reputation for itself for deep-sea sailors. All that gradually changed, and the village had a mixture like any other village with just the occasional one going to sea.

I was very proud of the name of Canvas Town, a name which arose because of the number of boats issuing forth from Sandwick. It was a great tradition to have, and those of us who listened to the tales of the sea in the ceilidh house had only one ambition, and that was to keep alive that tradition. We could hardly do anything else. The sea was in the blood, and how often did we hear those tales of going round Cape Horn on half rations, or hauling on the lee braces up to the waist in sea water! How often have I myself, in my boyish fancy, climbed those riggings and stood on a slender footrope out at the extremity of the yard as she rolled and wallowed as sails were being shortened in foul weather. To us as boys, these men were our heroes— and what boy did not want to do the same? But alas! Times change and those days are past.

Most of the houses carried relics of the sailing ships and trips to foreign lands: sets of wooden bowls from the Baltic countries and long narrow red jars filled with Rigabalsam;

fancy shells and ebony elephants from the tropics, flimsy silk shawls for the women folk. There might also be a half model of a full-rigged ship in a glass case hanging on the wall. Many of the sailors came home in the winter and spent some of their time making those models.

I remember that one house where we used to ceilidh had one of those models. It was a three-masted barque, and when the old tar was in the mood, out would come the pocket knife and, starting with the foresail, we had to repeat the names of each sail right up the foremast, mainmast and mizzen, including the jibs, stay sails and fore and afters. I knew them all when I was a boy of twelve.

My wife had heard these repeated so often that she too could not help learning them off by heart, and she knew all the types of ships by their rigs. I remember drawing her attention one day to a ship tacking against a headwind entering the harbour. I thought it was a brig, but she corrected me and told me it was a brigantine and was able to point out the difference. She remembered the first steamer that came into Stornoway harbour and how all the villagers were standing in the doorways looking at it.

As a young man, I remember standing on the lee side of a peatstack with some of the old sea rovers. They were all in their seventies or eighties and retired for some years from the sea. A beautiful ship in full sail had come round the point and was entering the harbour under the power of a small motor. A discussion soon arose as to what type of ship she was. She had three masts and was square on all three, but her fore, main and mizzen sails were all fore and aft. She had many other peculiarities which the critics did not like. Whatever name one suggested, the other would point out a sail which ruled out that category. Thus they exhausted all the types of sailing ships that they knew of and came to the conclusion that she was 'moffrigged'. I had never heard of this type before and asked old John what it meant. 'Oh, she is nothing at all,' he replied. 'But, surely a fine, beautiful ship like that is something,' I protested. 'No,' he insisted, 'she is nothing at all, a bit of everything; she is not a real ship.' John could not explain anything further and I became very curious to find out more. It took me some time to discover that 'moffrigged' was the sailor's description of 'hermaphrodite rigged', a term applied by seamen to any rig which did not conform to the recognised types.

Old John's great boast was that he was on the only sailing ship, the *Gleniffer*, which made the double crossing to the St. Lawrence and back in one season. I could not vouch for the truth of the statement, but John was quite proud of it.

I asked Murchadh Thomais one day while we were pulling our small boat out to the fishing grounds about two miles away what was the longest pull he ever had. 'It was when we got wrecked in the Straits of Belle Isle. We were rowing for three days before we were picked up,' he answered, apparently unconcerned. One sailor in the village had been given up as lost and his 'widow' wore mourning clothes for nearly two years. He had been wrecked on the island of Anticosti in the Gulf of St. Lawrence, and he had no means of letting his whereabouts be known. There were few houses which had not lost somebody in those days. They sailed and were never heard of again.

Oceangoing schooners were being built at this time at the Patent Slip in Stornoway, and some of them have sailed round the world. One house I knew of had an exact replica of one of these ships. This man had been serving his time as a carpenter at the slip, and for every plank that was fixed during the day, he placed the corresponding one in his model at night.

Canvas Town

There was hardly a house in the district but had a bundle of discharge papers. They were elaborately done and were not unlike five pound notes. One of my father's earlier ones interested me very much. It was from a ship called the *Daisy*, carrying a cargo of herring to the Baltic. The interesting thing was that the port of registry was given as Holm, a small village of ten houses then just two miles outside Stornoway. Surely Stornoway was the recognised port of registry then, or had it not yet come into the limelight? The old 'barracks' or curing station could still be seen at Holm. The place was ideal for landing fish as it stood on the narrow neck of Shildinish peninsula. Shelter was available in all weathers; if the wind was too strong on the south beach, they would land on the north beach, and vice versa. The village crofters used the old ruins as a dipping place for their sheep.

The first teapot to arrive in the village was taken home by one of the sailors. The same house also had a clock. This innovation placed them very high on the social scale. The neighbours were quite jealous of Peigi, and Peigi herself tended to hold her head in the air a bit. Relics of the old clan equality still existed in many parts of the isles, and one hardly dared to have anything that the rest did not have.

Peigi was very proud of her teapot, but alas! it did not reign very long. The usual crowd were in ceilidhing and Peigi was swanking her teapot. The house was the old-fashioned type of black house with the fire in the middle of the floor. The usual method for making tea was to pour the boiling water into the pot, take a red-hot ember from the peat fire, crush it down with the tongs and put the pot sitting on it for a good brew.

Peigi was wearing a skirt reaching down to her ankles, the kind with a pocket in the back and three or four rows of black braid at two-inch intervals round the hem. Some of the stitches in the lowest row had come loose and a loop or two of the braid was hanging down. She had just placed the teapot on the glowing embers and was turning to go away to attend to the teacups when Big Angus, who was always up to some tricks, saw his chance to bring Peigi back to the level of the rest of the community. Just as she was straight up, he adjusted the hanging loop over the spout of the teapot, rascal that he was! When poor Peigi turned to go, away came the teapot, which rolled over on its side throwing up a cloud of ashes far larger than any hen ever did when it flapped its wings by the fireside. The spout broke. Big Angus managed to suppress, though somewhat audibly, a smothered laugh through his nose. But nobody suspected him, and he was the one who was greatest in his sympathy for the tragedy. In spite of it all, the teapot saw service for many a day after that and, like many other Highland teapots of those happy days, lived to a ripe old age with neither spout nor handle. One wag in the district described a fat, chubby woman as having a face like the one you would see in the sides of a new teapot.

Any tales of Canvas Town's sailors would not be complete without mention of Coinneach Iain'ic Ruairidh, the most loved of all our sailors, Kenny Morrison. What a favourite he was with the boys! Coinneach got all his threshing done in the barn throughout the winter by the boys, who always flocked in and were entertained with sea tales and sea shanties. He also taught them how to make sennit with straw. Sennit is a flat braid normally made of rope.

Many steamers in the Baltic timber trade called at Stornoway in those days and always required a pilot to take them inside the harbour and alongside the coal hulk. Sandwick pilots had the advantage over the other villages as they could see the steamer long before the others. Whenever one came round Rudha na Circ (Chicken Head), there was a rush to the shore, down with the boat, and they were at the harbour entrance well before the steamer. Coinneach was usually the pilot. The usual pilotage was a couple of pounds and a bottle of brandy.

When the job was over, they retired to one of the local hotels to share out the money and the bottle of brandy. Probably a dram or two was taken out of the money before the share-out. They were good seamen and, even in an intoxicated condition, respected the sea and its ways. On one occasion, however, they tied the boat to a vertical iron ladder which was down the side of the pier. After the square-up in the hotel, they came down to the boat to go home, but by that time the tide had risen quite a few feet. Iain Dhomnuill climbed step by step down the ladder and didn't realise the water was so high until it was up to his neck!

One old salt I knew very well used to remark in true sailor language when asked how he was that day: 'Well, I am not too bad. I am here at the harbour bar with the pilot jack at the fore, waiting for the Pilot'.

3

ROADS AND TRANSPORT

There were only two kinds of road in the isles at the turn of the century—bad roads and worse roads! The former were the main roads connecting the villages with the towns and the latter mere inter-village tracks. And even the main roads were like old Gaul, divided into three parts, one where the horse walked in the middle of the road, the other two being the tracks left by the cart wheels. A high ridge separated the one from the other, and great care was needed when two carts met and had to go off the beaten track. Pedestrians preferred to take the cut across the moor because it was shorter and easier on the feet. That explains the comment by a local worthy that the people walked like goats through long practice on the 'no roads'.

The roads in many places had no bottoming and the soft peat came through in many places. They were repaired only once or twice per year, when the job was given to a local contractor whose only qualification was that he had a horse and cart and a sou'wester. Strangely enough, the road was more difficult to use after the repairs than before. Several cartloads of metal or shingle were spread along the wheel tracks to fill up the hollows.

I pitied the poor cyclist after the road was repaired, as the only part he could use was the wheel tracks about six inches wide. The first cycles I knew were old second-hand bone-shakers with a fixed driving wheel, no bell, no mudguards and often no brakes. The bell was of little use as the cows and sheep paid no heed to it anyway.

Brakes were hardly needed as the speed had to be dead slow. If brakes were needed, the boot was jammed on the top of the wheel at the front fork. The cycle was called in Gaelic *an each iaruinn*, the iron horse.

The main means of transport was the horse and cart. All long-distance travelling was by this method and later on by the gig. Even the postman had to walk long distances. In my own village of Sandwick, all the letters were left at the Mission House, where they were collected by the people. A letter might lie there for several days until someone told you that there was a letter for you. The postman for our district had a ten-mile journey. Later the people presented him with a pony and gig in recognition of his services, and if anyone ever deserved it, it was poor old George.

Latterly, the mails were delivered by fast motor early in the morning and a local postman made the delivery. He knew more about absent friends than anyone else in the village. 'Here is a letter from Uilleam in Toronto,' he would say as he handed it over, and might mention that Iain Thomais got one yesterday from his boy in Australia.

He could tell not only about letters but about parcels too. He knew that Mrs. Munro got a pair of new boots yesterday; that *bean* Iain would be getting window blinds. He knew that the long narrow parcels contained corsets, usually Spirella, and that Mor (Marion) got curtains from her daughter who was in service as a maid in Edinburgh.

C.O.D. parcels had no worries for the local postman. He delivered them all irrespective of whether he brought back the corresponding value or not. Perhaps *bantrach* Alasdair (Alex's widow) was in the peats or Kateag Uilliam was at Communion in the next parish; it made no difference. He was not going to carry all those parcels miles back again to the office. He knew they were safe and that he would get the money in due course.

A definite advance was made in transport when the gigs

arrived. The journey became shorter in time and the springs eased the jolting. But it was cold travelling. The Lewis gig had a seat across the middle and carried six passengers, three in front facing the horse, and three behind facing the opposite way. During the winter weather it was a relief to get out at each hill and walk up the brae. Many people, however, could not afford the fare and walked as usual.

One such person in one particular district was said never to have taken a hire. He always walked both ways. So when anyone in the district was going to walk to town, he said he was going to take 'gige Chalum', or, as it was called in the south, Shanks's pony.

The motor car changed completely the nature of travel in the isles. Roads had to be improved and the time factor was greatly shortened. I remember the first car that appeared in Lewis. Some sportsmen who had taken one of the lodges for shooting and fishing took a car to the island. It passed through our village on the Sabbath and that set more tongues wagging than the novelty of the car itself. It was sure to come to a bad end.

The boys raced it along the road for a mile outside the village and their curiosity was aroused by the lovely symmetrical designs the tyres left in the mud on the road. The people seemed antagonistic to anything on wheels on the Sabbath. One woman, the only one in the village to own a pram, dared to go out with it on Sunday. It was the main topic of conversation for many days to come and there was some talk of not giving her the baptism.

When the cars first arrived, they were the bane of the crofters' lives, particularly those of them who had horses. The animals did not understand what this strange thing was and showed signs of great fear. The moment a crofter saw one approaching, he immediately got out of the cart and turned the horse round the other way so that it could not see the car coming. The horse was backed into a dock or bank and a man on each side of the bridle hung on until the danger had passed.

Sometimes, however, the car appeared suddenly over the breast of a hill and there was no time to turn the animal around. The terrified creature made for the moor, often resulting in broken shafts or harness, and the crofter himself was lucky if he escaped unhurt. He usually found himself thrown into a peat bank. Things would not have been quite so bad if he had been able to vent his wrath on the offender, but the scoundrel was always about a mile down the road before the crofter recovered.

One such crofter, on recovering, saw a motorcycle following up the car that had ditched him and cried, 'Mo chreachsa thainig, am beil feaghainn og aca cuideachd?' (Woe is me, have they young ones as well?)

The local Territorials, who were at that time a mountain battery, took about thirty horses from Lewis to the annual training camp at Buddon. Things went all right until they got to their destination. The horses were all out of the train and were being led by the drivers from the station, when an express train whistled by on the off line. These horses had seen many cars but they had never seen such an infernal thing as this. In the twinkling of an eye, all ears were erect, all eyes wide open, and away they went all over the sands with their tails sticking almost straight in the air!

When the regulation was enforced that all carts had to carry the name of the owner, some crofters got into trouble with the law. One fellow who regularly came to town for a load of meal for the local merchant was stopped several times by the police for not having the name on his cart. He replied that he could not read or write, but his excuses were to no effect. He was told that if he did not have his name on the cart the next time he came to town, he would be charged.

On arriving home later that same evening, he reported the incident to the merchant and vowed he would not go back until the name had been put on. Some of the locals were ceilidhing (visiting) in the shop at the time and heard the story. Domhnull Mhurchaidh, who had the reputation of being one of the best-read men in the village, said he would put the name on for him. So he looked around the shop and saw an empty box lying in a corner and was soon out at the door nailing the end of the box on to the shaft. 'There you are now,' he said to the driver, 'you have the most stylish name plate in the district'. The plate had just one word on it, MARGARINE, in big black letters.

The following day, he made the usual trip to town. He felt in merry, defiant mood as he approached the town, sitting at the front of the cart with his legs dangling between the shafts. When he entered the town, two of the police met him. He could hardly miss them in such a small place. 'I see you have got your name plate up at last,' said one of them with a broad smile over his face. 'Who put it on for you?' 'One who knew better than either of you,' came the reply. And with that, he jerked the horse, leaving the two policemen staring after him at the sign.

The local policeman was also responsible for preventing cruelty to animals, and a regular SPCA man called once or twice each year to report. In this particular district, the local policeman was a tall, lean six-footer with hardly any fat on his body. The village blacksmith had an old mare which he kept for odd jobs, but she was in very poor condition, and the policeman said he would get into trouble if the 'Cruelty' saw her. So the day before the 'Cruelty' was due, he went up to the smiddy to warn the blacksmith to hide her out of the way until the rounds would be over. The blacksmith did not like his reference to 'that bag of bones' and swore the mare would be left where she was. And sizing up the policeman from head to foot, retorted sarcastically, 'We'll see what he will say about yourself first'.

Times have changed. Horses, the few that are around, do not shy away when they see a car. The cyclist races along on a tar-surfaced road. Nobody walks any distance, and it was only a question of time until Callum's gig belonged to the past.

4

Our Daily Bread

At the time of which I write, around 1900, in the main there was ample food, although the occasion arose when food went a little scarce, particularly when crops were bad. The scantiest time in the crofter's house was always the late spring, in the gap between the tail end of last year's crop and the following harvest.

This was a bleak period for the cattle also as the last year's stacks were exhausted and the new grass had not sprung. The economy was bad. Most crofters kept three or four cows and followers, and the croft was not big enough to keep them. He got a little milk from each, and it was arranged that the cows calved at different times during the year. That gave him milk all the year round. As a rule, there was no scarcity of milk, and if circumstances were such that the cows calved about the same time, the neighbours supplied all the requirements and not a penny was charged for it. Milk was not sold.

Latterly, the crofter kept one cow, but that was as good as the three he had before. The strain had improved and had a bigger milk yield. However, new methods often bring repercussions in other directions. Now he did not have enough manure to keep his soil fertile and had to resort to artificial manures. It eventually came to the situation where, in Lewis, milk had to be imported from the mainland as the island's supply did not meet the demand. The crofters who had an extra supply of milk found it difficult to move from the old tradition of not selling milk.

Our Daily Bread

In the old days, there was plenty of milk, much of it drunk by both young and old. There was no waste, and when milk went thick or sour, it was used for baking and drinking. There was always a large jugful of it or a bowl on the dresser, and it was a case of 'help yourself'.

Any surplus was turned into crowdie. The thick milk was put in a large pot and hung very high over a slow fire. The pot was kept just warm enough, and after some time the crowdie gathered on the top and the whey below. It was then lifted off with the hands and as much as possible of the whey squeezed out. Some squeezed all the whey out until what was left became a solid lump which, after some time, became cheese. Others preferred it not so dry and spread a thick covering of it on bread over butter. Nothing was more palatable than bread with fresh butter and a good thick covering of salted crowdie. The whey was not wasted either. It was used for baking and made excellent scones or oatcakes.

I have seen girls of twelve years baking the house requirements of flour bannocks on the old-fashioned girdle, each bannock about twelve inches across. They were then cut into four sections or scones, wrapped up in a clean towel and put out on the window sill to cool.

The girdle went out of fashion when the baker's van began calling at the village once or twice a week. The girdle reminds me of the story of a merchant in the isles who had a good-going business but who couldn't write. He did, however, keep a kind of cash book in which he drew the items given out on credit.

A crofter came in one day to pay his account and the cash book was consulted. 'You got a boll of meal.' 'Yes,' came the reply. 'You got a score of hooks.' 'That is right,' said the crofter. 'And a girdle.' 'No,' answered the crofter, 'I did not get a girdle.' 'But there it is,' insisted the merchant, pointing at the same time to a circle drawn in the book. The crofter was just as sure that he got no girdle, and after a pause, added, 'I got a Balmoral'. 'Good gracious,' said the merchant, 'that's it, right enough. I forgot to put the tourie in.' Wetting the pencil with his tongue, he proceeded to place a black dot in the middle of the circle!

The girdle was on the fire daily in the black house, and eight or nine bannocks, according to the size of the family, was a day's baking. The oatcakes took a little more time and skill. One side was baked on the girdle and the other was toasted to a nice brown against the fire or put over the embers on the brander.

Cooking over an open fire naturally had its disadvantages. The chain or *slabhraidh* on which the pots were hung was well covered with soot down to within a foot or two of the fire. The falling soot, as already mentioned, ruined many a good meal. A lid or plate therefore covered all the pots on the fire, but with all the care in the world, sometimes the inevitable happened. The porridge needed to be stirred, or the soup needed salt, and during that brief moment, down would come a lump of soot. Fortunately, the soot was dry and could be skimmed off with a clam shell; nevertheless, many a meal was eaten tasting of soot.

Breakfast in the main consisted of porridge and milk, good solid, thick porridge with lumps in it. Sometimes the children preferred treacle with the porridge. A spoonful was taken out of the middle of the plate, and the 'hole' was filled with treacle. Spoonful after spoonful was then taken, dipped in the treacle and eaten. I remember as children the delight it gave us to make black patterns of treacle on the top of the porridge with the dripping spoon. Bread and milk or tea were taken after the porridge.

Many people made brose in the morning. It was easily done and very sustaining. To make it, boiling hot water was poured over the raw oatmeal in a bowl until it formed a thick dough.

Dinner was usually potatoes and fish. Fish was plentiful, and if the season was good, the crofter with a good store of potatoes and a barrel of salt herring in his barn had no fears for the winter. The quantity of potatoes one could consume with salt herring was amazing. A large potful was easily devoured by three or four people. With meat, a potato or two would suffice, but with herring, one just went on until they were finished.

The peelings and herring bones were kept and mixed up with bran or thirds and given to the cattle or hens. No knives or forks were used with potatoes and herring, and I would say to the uninitiated, if you want to get the proper flavour of potatoes and herring, do not use a knife and fork; use your fingers!

Sometimes the potatoes were mashed and served with milk. A large, heaped plateful was put in the centre of the table. Each person was served with a bowl of milk, and each spoonful of potato was dipped in the milk and eaten. Sometimes the cold potatoes would be sliced and fried.

It was customary to kill a young bullock or sheep in the winter. The meat was salted and dried and used with the potatoes during the winter. Even when the wartime restrictions were on, quite a few sheep were hanging by the hind legs in the barn without any permit having been obtained. Much of the town supply of meat was imported from the mainland. One village butcher who was getting a supply from Dingwall wired to his agent there that he was not to send on any meat the following week as he now had a permit for killing himself!

The intestines of all slaughtered animals were used. They were cleaned and filled up with barley or oatmeal, suet, blood and seasonings to make blood puddings. These were boiled first, after which they were sliced and fried. They were delicious.

Broth was the commonest soup—real thick stuff with plenty of cabbage, turnip and peas. After-dinner puddings were rare except at weddings. One crofter referred to cornflour as *lite bainnse*, or wedding porridge.

At suppertime it was a case of pot luck. Some people preferred their porridge or their potatoes and herring at night. Probably the most popular dish of all was the *ceann cropaic* or stapped head. (Stapped was pronounced as stappit.) This was a haddock head, or better still, a cod or ling's head, filled up with a mixture of fish liver and oatmeal. The gills were taken out and the head filled with the mixture. It was then boiled along with the fish. The stomach of the cod or ling was also filled with the same mixture and boiled. It was delicious to eat, and I know of nothing richer in vitamins, as in the cooking it sweated beads of oil.

In the city, ling was rarely seen in the fishmonger's; cod was in greater demand. Yet in the isles the fishermen would seldom take cod if they could get ling. The ling is a much cleaner-living fish, as can be seen from the contents of the stomach. The cod is a scavenger and will eat practically anything. I do not wish to put people off their cod steaks by divulging some of the things I have seen in the stomachs of cod!

As previously mentioned, when fish was plentiful, it was salted and dried. Most houses had a *cluaran* or dried thistle. When seasoned and dried, the thistle retained its shape and became hard like wood, making a handy stand for hanging smaller fish such as whiting, haddock or saith. They hung from a beam or from the wall, and a fish hung from every limb or branch of the thistle. During the darkness, the phosphorus on the fish shone, making the thistle look like a fairy Christmas tree.

Our Daily Bread

One time I visited an old man of eighty in the village of Lochganvich, one of the only two inland villages in Lewis. While we waited for tea to brew, he went out to the cornyard, pulled out a sheaf or two and stripped the seed off. These he placed in an old three-legged pot over a fire in the barn in order to harden the seed.

He had an old hand quern with which he ground his oats into meal. He served this in a bowl mixed with cream—straight from the stack to the table. I examined the contents of the table, and only two items, the tea and the sugar, were bought. He had his own butter, crowdie, eggs, scones and oatcake and, of course, the *ulag* or mixture of cream and oatmeal.

In those days, every crofter took a quantity of oats to the mill and would be back with several bolls of meal. Each village had its own kiln for hardening the grain before milling. The kiln was just a small bothy with iron plates a few feet above the fire. The grain was spread over the plates and hardened with the heat of the fire. It was an all-night job and the young lads and lassies looked forward to the night at the kiln.

All the threshing was done with the *suist* or flail. Experts travelled from village to village, and for a small sum and their keep, undertook all the threshing. About a dozen sheaves, six on each side and the seed end in the middle, were laid on the floor. The steady measured thump, thump of the flail could be heard all day. It was heavy work. At night the barn was lit dimly by the tinker's lamp, a slight improvement on the old crusie. It had a conical container for the oil and a wick of cotton rag through the top. It had no globe and emitted lots of smoke.

Other crofters threshed their own day by day. They would open a few sheaves and slash small wisps of it over the mouth of an empty barrel. The seed fell into the barrel. The flail received its death blow when the hand threshing mill came along. The year's threshing could be done by it in one day. It had a handle on each side and needed a crew of four, and one person feeding, to work it. The seed fell through a grating to a tarpaulin on the floor, and the straw was thrown out at the rear. It was very heavy work, but it was great fun chasing the girls with mice and putting some of them into the men's pockets. There was a great deal of excitement when the stack was nearly finished, particularly if there was a rat there. Everybody was on his toes; even the dogs knew, and the rat seldom got away.

Such is a general outline of the Hebridean diet of over eighty years ago. With the change in diet the physique of the race has changed too. The plates may have been chipped and the cups or teapot may not have had a handle, but without fail, grace was said before and after each meal, thanks given to God with full humility for the blessing He had bestowed upon them, even although, according to modern standards, it was dangerously near the poverty line at times.

5

OATMEAL

If ever there was anything in Scotland that demanded a national memorial, surely that would be oatmeal. Where would our country be, or what would we do without porridge? But like many good Scottish customs, the uses of oatmeal are, sorry to relate, a thing of the past. It was used in many forms in the Highlands—*lit* (porridge), *brochan, stiuireag, stapag, fuarag, ulag, deoch bhan* (various names for gruel), and *aran corc* (oat bread).

Porridge, of course, was the main diet and was taken with milk or treacle. The latter was never taken if milk was available, but sometimes the cows went dry, and although neighbours were very kind, there just wasn't any milk to be had. Before plates became fashionable, the porridge was poured out on a big *clar* or tray. A bowl of milk was given to each person and each spoonful of porridge was dipped into the bowl. Later, the bowl was discarded and one half of the porridge in the plate was lifted with the spoon on top of the other half and the milk poured into the empty space.

We as children preferred lumpy porridge. To make good porridge, the pot must be stirred most of the time and salt should be added during that stage. Salt added afterwards does not give the same taste—and porridge without salt is tasteless. There is a Gaelic proverb concerning anything you dislike very much: 'B'fhearr leam lite gun salainn', meaning 'I would prefer porridge without salt'.

One author on Scottish affairs stated that porridge

should be called 'them'. I do not wish to confuse the issue, but we always called 'them' 'it', and, as the gender of porridge in Gaelic is feminine, 'it' or 'them' was sometimes referred to as 'she'!

Another form in which oatmeal was used a great deal was *brochan* and *prois*. The former should not be confused with porridge, because what we call *brochan* in Lewis is not porridge. In some other isles, *brochan* is porridge, but in Lewis this was a thin mixture of oatmeal and water with a pat of butter thrown in. It was supped hot out of a bowl like gruel.

All the others- *stapag, fuarag,* etc. -were combinations of the same thing. The *stiuireag* was a mixture of oatmeal, warm water and salt to taste. The *deoch bhan* (pale drink) was a fistful or two of oatmeal poured into a pail of water for drinking at the peats or anywhere away from the drinking water supply. The *ulag* was served with a meal and consisted of oatmeal and cream supped with a spoon from a bowl. Brose was a hurried meal and was made by pouring boiling hot water over the oatmeal until it became a stiff paste. Salt was added to taste. It could be made very hurriedly and was most sustaining.

Like the average Highlander, porridge has also degenerated! It can be practically anything today. I have seen it poured from a jug on the breakfast table like milk and even served with fruit, but the porridge of my youth was a good thick one which gave asthmatic wheezy groans from the pot as if it had difficulty in breathing. As one crofter put it, 'I have no use for the porridge that mutters in a thin voice, 'Mise is thusa, mise is thusa' (me and you, pronounced meesha sussa). Give me the pot that groans, 'Mi fhein, pech, mi fhein, pech''. This indicated good thick stuff panting for breath! It was often said that porridge was no use unless the spoon could stand up in it without support. I am afraid that if our forebears saw what is called porridge today, they would decide that they were far better off where they were!

One family I knew had porridge every morning for breakfast, and the scraping of the pot was given to the one who was finished first. Whenever the reward fell to Iain, he could be seen sitting on the *starran* (flagstone over the front door drain) with the *pulais* (handle) of the three-legged pot round his neck. The pot was sitting on his chest, and he was ready to repel all invaders!

During the lean days, many people had nothing at all along with the porridge, but it must have been worse in the earlier generation. The remark of one parent to her boy who was complaining that there was no milk with the porridge at least suggests this, as she said, 'You should be grateful that you have a clean spoon with it'.

Domhnull Ossian was removed in his old age to the Big House, the local name for the Poor House (or old folks' home). When out for a walk one day, he met one of his old neighbours from the village. The neighbour asked all the usual questions as to how he liked the new house and what kind of food they were getting. Domhnull told him every-thing was all right except the porridge. 'It would run,' he said, 'from here to the lighthouse on a plank.'

In those days, each village had its own kiln and each district its own mill for grinding. The *ath* or kiln was a small bothy or outhouse built on the same principles as the black house. The roof was thatched and a large perforated iron plate was fixed a few feet above the fireplace. The grain was spread out on the iron plate and a good fire was kept going all night. Occasionally, the grain was raked backwards and forwards. The young folk always looked forward to the night at the *ath*, where the time was spent in telling old tales and singing.

The purpose of the *tireadh* was to harden the grain. If this was not done, the mill would not make such a good job of the grinding and the meal would be soft and flaky. The hardened grain ground more easily and made better meal. All the residue was saved and taken home, and it was later given to the cattle. A type of porridge known as *laghan* was made from the mill residue. All the mills were water-driven. I doubt if any of these mills are in existence today, and the only mill I know of in the island is power-driven.

Every house one entered had a row of meal bags along the side of the room, usually on the settle. The meal was kept in a warm place to avoid deterioration. It was all barley and oatmeal. Flour was more or less unknown in rural Lewis at this time (before the turn of the century). An old man told me that he was ten years of age before he tasted flour. A ship had gone ashore in Stornoway harbour with a cargo of wheat grain, and the damaged cargo was being sold off cheaply in the town. This man's father had bought several bags and, after hardening it in the kiln, took it to the mill to be ground, but the mill could only grind it down to a fine oatmeal consistency, so it was not really flour but wheaten meal.

Aran corc or oat bread was, of course, a large part of the diet. Bannocks of it about ten inches across and half an inch thick could be seen toasting at every fire. Earlier, the brander was used for toasting. It was rectangular and consisted of thin iron bars about an inch apart and resting on four small legs three or four inches high. Red-hot embers of peat were broken down and put underneath. The last brander I saw in use was as a small boy of about ten years of age, around 1900.

There were various kinds of bannocks; some were made with just oatmeal, some had eggs and some had fish liver. The *bonnach oraidh* (golden bannock) contained eggs and got its name probably from the golden colour given to the bannock by the eggs. Whoever was the first to report to the owner the arrival of a newborn lamb or calf got a *bonnach oraidh* as his reward.

Barley bannocks were not too popular. They tended to be tough and leathery. A barley bannock seemed to go well with salt herring. At any rate, there wasn't much choice, and people were very glad to have it at times.

With the introduction of electricity, the old-fashioned girdle probably disappeared. Even before the power arrived, the girdle (or gridle, as some term it) was going out of fashion. The baker's van coming to the villages several times in the week with all kinds of fancy pastries helped deliver the death blow. And no wonder the old crofter said to his wife when he saw the van coming along the street, 'Anna, so a ghraeideil a tighinn' ('Annie, here's the girdle coming!').

6

THE LEAN DAYS

The summer visitor to the isles might have received the impression that it was a land flowing with milk and honey, and perhaps it was so at that time. But do not let us forget that the isles have also had their lean periods. The leanest time was always the late spring, as by that time the hay and corn stacks had practically disappeared and the new grass had hardly begun to grow, the store of potatoes had dwindled down to nothing, and even the fish had forsaken the shores for deeper waters and the urge to spawn. Those were indeed lean days for man and beast.

The cattle as a rule were inside all winter except on the rare occasions when the weather was suitable. They were allowed out then 'to move their legs'. There was little for them to eat in any case, and they loitered around the cornstacks looking for any break in the fences to get through. Some of them were good at this and developed a village reputation. They would be chased from one corn stack to another and might just as well have been tied up in the byre.

Most crofters were overstocked with animals and the croft simply could not yield sufficient to sustain them. During bad winters the cows had a very hard time, and on their first appearance out in the spring, found it difficult to walk. In fact, some of them had to be helped out.

The soil was poor and had to be heavily manured. Long years of intensive cultivation had taken the best out of the soil, and as many cattle as possible had to be kept in order to get sufficient manure. Latterly, the average crofter kept one cow which yielded as much as the three kept by his grandfather. Nor did he need all the manure that was needed by his grandfather, as with his knowledge of the rotation of crops and the use of artificial manures he was able to keep his land in good trim.

Most crofters in my district (Sandwick) took home a cartload or two of fish heads or fish bones. These were heaped up on the croft somewhere at the back of the house and covered over with a thick layer of peat dross. In the springtime the heap was turned over and the dross well mixed with the decayed offal. There was an almost unbearable smell from it and steam rose from it in the turning. The mixture was spread very thinly over the oats and it yielded a heavy crop. Later, this practice was stopped because many maintained it forced the soil too much and no new humus was being formed.

The cattle got their share of the potatoes as long as they were available. The potato peelings and general household scraps were kept and mixed with bran or thirds, and that made one meal at least along with the usual quota of straw. Many crofters could not afford bran or thirds and they relied on the residue from the grinding of their oats at the local mill. A curly seaweed which grows near the highwater mark, *feamainn chirea*, was gathered, boiled and given to the cows. If the weather was mild and the cows were out, they usually made for the shore and chewed away most of the time at the tangle.

The household in general were also short during the lean days, and it was a welcome day when the potato pit was to be opened. The potato pit was sacred and in no circumstances would it be touched until sowing time. It held that season's seed and could not be encroached on. Nevertheless, there were extras in the pit. Some potatoes would be too big for planting, and even if they were cut up according to the number of eyes, a large portion of the potato might still be left. Some potatoes were also 'blind', without eyes, and some may have had a spot of disease. These provided enough for a few days at least during the lean times. The hens perhaps fared worst of all, for they were thrown entirely on their own resources.

Most of the potatoes were split up for planting, leaving two or three eyes in each section. The splitting was done by the women, and an odd saucerful of lime was thrown over the potato pieces in the creel. There was a quota of creels each household planted per season. Great care had to be taken when the pit was opened.

In the stackyard there was the same scarcity. Sheaf by sheaf had been drawn until nothing was left but a mere skeleton of a stack. In the olden days it was customary to put a *cragan* of butter in the bottom of the stack in the autumn when it was plentiful. This was to ensure a supply of butter in the lean days when they reached the bottom of the stack in the springtime.

Whether it was caused by hunger or not, many Lewis cows chewed clothes, and women had to be on the alert if they had washing on the green or the line. Some of the heifers would spend a whole day, if they were not disturbed, chewing away at a pair of pants, a sheet or a towel. Some of them even chewed old boots, and probably, as most of the boots in those days were made of gutta percha, the modern craze for chewing gum is just an imitation of what the Lewis cow was doing a century ago!

Our croft at home measured one and a half acres. There was a short frontage to the road and the rest was two long ribbons of *feannags* about a quarter of a mile in length. The women folk knew its length as they had to carry all the winter manure on their backs in a creel all that distance. The men used barrows, and that wasn't any easier, for it was a stiff push uphill all the way. We did the whole lot at first with the spade, but latterly ploughing became fashionable. It was a day's work for a pair of horses to plough it, sow the oats and harrow it. The young boy of the family got the job of following the plough and picking up all the potatoes unearthed by the plough. A few pailfuls were picked up in this way and were always a welcome contribution to the larder at this time.

The usual yield in my district was eight to one in bulk. But in good machair land it could be as high as ten or twelve to one. In those days, it was common to harvest over a hundred creels of potatoes. A creel was about a hundredweight (or 112 pounds) or more according to the size of the creel.

Some crofts had the *brisgean* or silver weed. As children we always watched when these crofts had the plough as we got an ample supply of *brisgean* that day. I am afraid we were not too hygienic about cleaning them. We rubbed them against our trousers or jersey and munched away at them. Sometimes we took them home and singed them over a peat ember. It was white inside and brittle, and as far as I remember, was really quite tasteless. We also ate *buineagan* or sorrel. They were very sour and made you screw up your face.

The lean days were soon forgotten when the machair was in bloom, when the fish came back again, and the music of the sheiling was once more heard. *Faire, faire!* In spite of the lean days, those were happy times.

7

OUR CLOTHES

It is believed by many that all Highlanders wear the kilt, that they roam the hillsides with the heather between their toes, brandishing a claymore and nursing a bottle of Cream of the Barley fresh from the illicit still down the glen. The pity of it all is that it is not true! Indeed, I could count on one hand the number of people I saw wearing the kilt in the isles during my residence there, and those who did wear it were visitors or tourists. As for the claymores, there is no more thatch to hide them, and the still in the glen is as still as the glen itself. One or two loyal crofters I knew who wore the Glengarry were scorned and referred to as Rob Roys. The people in the isles did not worry much about dress and certainly not about fashion, and anyway, fashions were well out of date before they reached the remote isles in those days.

All married women wore the mutch. It was an unwritten law that all other forms of headdress had to be discarded on marriage. The *curag* or mutch gave a calm, natural dignity to the wearer. Much time was spent on the goffering of the mutch and most houses had an *iarunn caol* (narrow iron) or goffering iron. It was in size and shape like a test tube fixed to an iron base by a goose-neck stem. A long iron spike was first heated in the fire and pushed into the tube to give the necessary heat. Then the curls of white ribbon which adorned the front of the mutch were pressed around the tube. The starch enabled the beautiful trimming to remain firm. Manufactured starch had found its way to the isles at this time, but many people were not too familiar with its use and preferred to use their own home-made starch from potatoes. Hair styles did not change. The hair was parted in the middle and gathered in a cue or bun at the back of the head. The 'crowning glory' was never cut, and anyone doing so was looked upon as being common.

At work on the croft or about the house the women wore a *beannaig*. This was a large handkerchief folded diagonally and tied round the head and under the chin, as women sometimes do today. So, evidently, instead of being behind the times with styles and fashion, the isles appear to have been half a century ahead!

Earrings were worn by both sexes, not because it was considered stylish or fashionable but because they were reported to be good for weak eyes. Earrings which clipped on were no use as the important point as regards weak eyes was the piercing of the ear lobes. Indeed, many people had their lobes pierced who did not wear earrings at all. Probably, many people suffered from weak eyes because of the blanket of peat smoke which always filled the black house. The occupants got quite accustomed to it but strangers emerged with streaming eyes.

For torso wear the women wore a tight-fitting polka with a long row of buttons down the front. Blouses buttoning at the back would have been very inconvenient as all the babies were breast fed. The people dressed for warmth and comfort rather than style and fashion. The thick, heavy skirt which reached down to the heels had several rows of black braid along the lower hem. In the back of the skirt was a pocket, which usually contained a handkerchief, a key, a reel (spool) on a string and probably some peppermints. As boys we always knew when we saw granny's hand fumbling for the back pocket that something nice was forthcoming.

There was no dainty underwear in those days. Underneath the thick heavy skirt was the *cota strianach* or striped skirt and the *cota ban* or white skirt. The outer skirt was rolled up to form a *dronnag* for the creel. The creel rested on the *dronnag* and a good *dronnag* meant a comfortable load rather than a chafed back. The *iris* or strap went round the chest and this left the hands free for knitting.

Dark stockings were worn by the younger women and white ones by the older ones. The stockings reached the knee, where they were tied by a garter of string or a thin strip of cotton material, and as the skirts were worn level with the heels, the garters could not be seen. One old woman who chewed tobacco regularly kept it in her stocking above the garter.

Most people had boots of some kind, but I do remember seeing the *cuarain*. They were old strips of woollen or cotton rags which were wound round and round the foot until the whole foot was covered up to the ankle. It was a long, tedious business getting them on and off. Hence the Gaelic proverb. 'feumaidh fear nan cuarain eirigh uair roimh fhear nam brog' (the man with the *cuarain* must get up an hour before the man with the boots). The *cuarain* should not be confused with *bonnagan* and *osanan*. The *cuarans* were for all-day use and served the same purpose as boots do today. The *bonnag* was an ordinary stocking cut at the ankle, the lower part used in the same way as ankle hose are worn now. The *osan*, on the other hand, was composed of the whole stocking with the sole cut away. The bare sole of the foot was on the ground and the rest of the leg was covered up to the knee. The *osan* was used mainly at the peats or when 'putting out the manure'. The ground underfoot at both these jobs was soft and pleasant to walk on and it was much cooler than if boots were worn. Women visiting relatives in villages many miles apart wore the *osan* all the way and walked on the grass verge by the roadside. When going to town it was customary to wear the *osan* until they were on the outskirts of the town where the *osan* was exchanged for boots. The same procedure was followed on the way back. The boots were only worn during their short stay in town.

Shoes were not very fashionable. Lacing boots were preferred. This is explained by the fact that the people spent much of their time on the moor rounding up sheep or taking home the cattle. Shoes, therefore, were not of much use to them as they were too low to keep out the water on an ever wet moor. After the lacing boots, elastic-sided boots became fashionable and were worn to church on Sundays and to prayer meetings. Later, some of the girls who followed the fishing as splitters and gutters to the east coast of Scotland and England took home buttoned boots which were considered to be the height of fashion.

8

THE VILLAGE SCHOOL

The village school was situated at the extreme east end of the village, in order to be more central for the children from Melbost, who had to travel over a mile from the opposite direction. There was a road to the school which these children could take but it was the long way round, and they preferred taking the short way over a stretch of wet, marshy moorland.

The school opened at ten o'clock in the morning, and the ringing of the school bell which hung in a small belfry at the gable end could be heard a long way off. From March to October practically all the children were barefoot and also bareheaded. The children who had to come from the remoter villages could not get home for dinner, and the piece of oatcake or scone they took with them for a 'play piece' was often eaten long before playtime. Large hard biscuits could be bought in the local village shop for a halfpenny—if you had one.

Each pupil had to carry a peat to school each day, for if you did not, you would not be allowed near the fire. Peats were plentiful, but carrying one on a cold, frosty morning with numbed fingers was not very pleasant. Many of the boys, however, did not carry one from home as there were many peatstacks on the way to school, and one occasional peat would not be missed. When all the odd peats came out of the one stack, however, and that was the one nearest to the school, the drain was soon felt. That was the reason why

The Village School

Alasdair Enag stood by his peatstack every morning until the school had gone in.

On entering the main door of the school, you came into a porch where rows of pegs indicated that it was a place for hanging coats or caps. We had neither, and the pegs in the boys' end were always empty. The girls, who occupied the same porch, were more fortunate, for an odd peg was occupied at their end.

There were only two rooms, which were large, spacious, uncomfortable and cold. Each room had one fireplace, with a large wooden box beside it. Every boy as he came in banged his peat with all his might against the side of the box as if glad to get rid of it, and also to draw the master's attention to the fact that he had brought one.

The desks were about fourteen feet long with no back supports. Usually eight boys sat at each desk. There were holes for inkwells, but they were always empty as the boys used to take them home for drinking cups for the birdcage.

There was also a long groove in the desk for slate pencils, and a slot in front to hold the slate. The desk itself was carved all over with names. Probably every boy who ever passed through the school aspired at least to have his initials or his nickname carved on his desk and slate. The slates were squared on one side and plain on the other. Sometimes we were allowed to take them home, usually before the estimated time of the inspector's visit, in order to scrub down the wooden frame.

The girls were more hygienic than the boys, for they always carried a wet rag to clean their slates. The boys just spat on theirs and gave it a good rub with the right sleeve. The result was that the jerseys, which nearly all boys wore, showed first signs of wear on the right sleeve.

On the floor of the room were flat, holed iron plates at intervals of about twelve feet, and a gale of wind blew up through them. Punishments included standing for a period on the ventilator. The master also used a cane about three feet long and half an inch in diameter, and its swish could be heard cutting the air before making contact with the hand. It always left a mark but nobody seemed to worry, it being considered good for one to get a good thrashing. A revolt by a pupil was an unheard-of thing, and parents never complained. In fact, the great ideal was to take what was coming without wincing.

The ventilators had another purpose, however, as they offered a fine receptacle to drop the hated cane through, down below the floor. The opportunities were many and they were always taken, so that the floor ventilators became a veritable canes' graveyard!

There seemed to be no scale of punishments; it all depended on the master's temper. I remember, as a boy of nine, getting three on each hand for having my eyes open at the prayer, and I had sufficient sense to realise that the master's eyes must have been open also or he could not have seen me.

When the schools first opened in Lewis, shortly after the passing of the Act of 1872, all the young men went to school. An old gentleman of my acquaintance told me that he went to his own village school when it was first opened.

One Sunday, two boys were seen playing on the shore. It was, of course, reported to the headmaster, who decided to make an example of them. On Monday morning, he ordered the two culprits out to the middle of the floor. He then got the two biggest boys in the school to take them round the classes on their backs so that every other boy could spit on their faces.

One of the big boys was the school bully and he simply delighted in this job. Each boy did what he was told, but when it was the turn of Seumas, who was no friend of the bully, he rolled his tongue backwards and forwards several times in his mouth to gather a big spit. Then, deliberately missing his aim, clapped it with deadly accuracy into the bully's face!

Language was a constant difficulty. The native language was Gaelic but the medium of instruction was English. We could say only 'yes' and 'no' in English, and often didn't know what the teacher was talking about. The result was that when we left school, some of us had only English gibberish or an anglicised Gaelic. Naturally, we thought in Gaelic and translated into English, and this explains how English constructions used by Gaelic speakers sounded so odd and strange to English ears. Gaelic is full of idioms which when translated literally make very comic English.

Uilleam was plodding through his arithmetic questions, and not doing so badly until he came to averages. The teacher tried his best to explain what 'on an average' meant, but the 'on' seemed to stump William. At last, the teacher asked him in Gaelic, 'Have you got hens at home?' 'Yes,' came the reply. 'Are they laying?' 'Yes' came the answer again. 'Well,' explained the teacher, 'suppose your mother went to the barn on Monday and got five eggs, on Tuesday two, Wednesday six, Thursday four, and Friday three. Now that is twenty eggs she would get in five days.' 'Yes,' replied William. 'That is just the same as if she got four eggs regularly every day, isn't it?' 'Yes,' again muttered William. 'Well then, we say your mother was getting four eggs on an average each day. Do you now follow what we mean when we say on an average?' William nodded but knew that their hens did not lay 'on an average'. 'What is meant now by on an average?' Poor William answered, 'The boxes the hens lay the eggs in'. The teacher, exasperated, told him he had a head like a pot of porridge.

Holidays were arranged to fit in with peat-cutting, sowing and harvest. A 'whipper-in' went round the houses each day to ask why John or Murdo was not at school. He had a notebook in which he wrote down all the excuses. It was indeed a strange collection—'watching the baby, mother in peats, gathering winkles, in town with father's dinner, ploughing the croft, trousers being washed'.

Boots were a luxury and were only worn in winter. In many cases, one was better without them because the boys waded through all the puddles and had wet feet all day. On receipt of a new pair of boots, the first test was to wade into a deep pool and see up to how many eyelets they were watertight. And proud was he who had one more row of tacks in the sole than the other boys!

Laces went in tatters in a very short time, and as the lace got shorter, there was not enough of it left to put a running knot on it, so a 'granny' was the easiest, and it never opened. But there was a time of reckoning at bedtime. Wading in the puddles all day soaked and swelled the laces, with the result that the 'granny' was as tight as if Samson himself had pulled the ends together.

The handiest marlin spike was a fork from the table drawer or from the box on the dresser. A prong of the fork would be squeezed between the strands of the knot and an attempt made to loosen them. Invariably, there was only one solution and that was to cut it. And so the laces got shorter and shorter, until finally, there was only sufficient left to tie the two holes at the top. Sometimes we raided the small line, which was hanging in hanks on the loft. One snood would do for both boots, and it would not be missed before the following spring. We were always prepared for a court martial at that time.

The examination day was a field day and we all looked forward to it. The inspectors arrived then, as now, un-announced. But surprise visits did not work in the isles at that time. There was only one way in those days of arriving and that was by the boat at night. Practically everybody went down to see who was coming off the boat and to get that morning's papers. The inspectors, of course, were well known and word went around the island by next morning that they had arrived. So, every scholar was in his place and the school looked a hive of industry.

The girls were nicely dressed for the occasion with clean white pinnies and coloured ribbons in their hair. The boys gave the boots their annual overhaul. And what a job! The blackening was usually as hard as a brick, so you spat and spat on it until some adhered to the brush. The boots had to be dried at the fire, and finally some kind of polish was achieved. When there was no blackening, sugar and milk were put in a saucer and used instead.

There were no motor cars in those days, so the inspectors had to hire a trap for long distances, and all distances were long in the isles. As a rule, they were taken into the schoolhouse for their lunch. The classes were examined one by one, and everybody passed. The ultimate aim was to get the Merit Certificate. The staff had no secondary or college education as we know it today, yet it was amazing the number of boys and girls from the isles who reached executive posts all over the world.

9

THE SABBATH DAY

There is a proverb in the isles which says 'As long as a Communion Sunday'. And all Sundays were long days in the isles when there was very little or nothing to do except attend the services. In my youth around the turn of the century, it was a day of worship, when the influence of the church was very strong and one dared not do otherwise even if one felt like it. Today it is more or less a day of rest and some people are daring to do small jobs on the Lord's Day.

In my youth, Sunday began a long time before midnight on Saturday. If it was near the Sabbath, no job was started. On the Saturday the usual activities went on plus all the necessities for Sunday. All the boots were brushed and polished for the services, and a double supply of potatoes, peats and food was taken in. As children, we had to take a double supply of water from the well. It meant four or five trips to the well with two large zinc pails and filling up the big earthenware jar or all the pots and pans in the house. The large wooden hoop which we placed over the pails eased the awkwardness of carrying two brimming pails. On stormy days a wisp of hay or straw was put in the pails to prevent the wind blowing the water out of the pails.

The potatoes and vegetables (cabbage and turnip) were washed and prepared ready to be hung over the fire on Sunday. Practically everybody went to church except the person in charge of the dinner. Most houses had sheep's head broth that day. The head was first singed over the face with red hot tongs and then split up the front with an axe. The brains were smeared over the face.

Knives and forks were becoming a little more plentiful and most houses had at least two or three of each. At times, the knives could not be found—Granny had one in the barn cutting potatoes and forgot to bring it back; Murdo had another one shaping a block of wood into a boat, etc. Often have I heard my mother say, 'The knife I had this morning cannot be found anywhere'. The fork was, as a rule, all twisted, having been used as a marlin spike by Norman or John to open that terrible knot in the bootlaces which had become so tightened by water.

Potatoes were usually served in their jackets. It was a sin to peel them before they went in the pot but not a sin to peel them after cooking. The children all hated broth and supped small spoonfuls round the edges. There was not much meat on a sheep's head, but a trotter was a fine thing to get your teeth into.

Immediately after dinner we all went to the Sunday school, where we were taught to read the Bible in Gaelic, sing psalms and learn the Shorter Catechism from cover to cover, including the grace before and after meat. I don't know if there is a longer Catechism, but the short one felt long enough! We also used to save the peas from the broth and throw them at each other when an opportunity was favourable.

There were times, however, when we managed to slip away from the rigours of the Sabbath and played away from prying eyes down on the sands, where we played football with a fisherman's cork, ate dulse or climbed the rocks in search of sea birds' nests. Sometimes these de-predations were reported to our parents and *diluain a bhreabain* awaited us on the Monday morning. *Diluain a bhreabain* means Monday of the kicks. It was a sin to chastise or punish on the Sabbath, and perhaps that was a good thing because the time lag helped to cool frayed tempers and gave parents time to weigh and consider, and even sometimes forget, the impending punishment.

Grace was said before and after each meal, and I have seen old crofters, even before drinking a glass of milk, lay their cap reverently to one side and first ask a blessing. Family worship was held in every house at night before retiring to bed, a chapter was read and a portion was sung, and everybody knelt down on the clay floor while the parent prayed and thanked God for the mercies He had provided that day. They had no luxuries but were grateful for the smaller mercies. It was customary then for neighbours to shake hands with each other when they met each morning and ask each other, 'A fhuair sibh tamh an raoir?' (Did you have peace last night?)

Everybody stayed indoors on Sunday and read the Bible or *Turus a Chriosdaidh* (*The Pilgrim's Progress*). There was no ceilidhing that day. Cattle and sheep, of course, had to be attended to and herding had to be done, but these were works of necessity and mercy. It was a sin to walk through the croft and see how the crops were getting on. I knew one ardent churchman who used to take the fly paper down on Sunday. He maintained it was a sin to have it trapping flies on the Lord's Day. Another kept the rooster under a creel on Sunday because he thought it wrong for the bird to be amongst the hens on that day.

I remember once being chastened by a deacon for not being at the morning service. Jokingly, I answered that I had listened to an excellent service that morning over the radio. 'How,' he retorted, 'can a service coming out of a wooden box have any spiritual value?' Old traditions and methods die hard, and great courage was required by any person in those isolated communities who desired to break away from them.

I knew of one girl who was teaching in a village several

miles from Stornoway, where her home was. She lodged in the village during the school week and cycled home for the weekends. This involved cycling back to the village every Sunday evening. The landlady took strong objection to this and told her if it did not stop she would have to look for other lodgings. The teacher remonstrated with her, but to no avail.

About the same time, a communion was being held in the district and a motor car arrived with the presiding ministers on the Sunday. 'What,' asked the teacher, 'is the difference between me cycling on the Sunday and the ministers arriving in a car?' 'A big difference,' came the reply. 'The ministers do not have to work their legs in a car the same as you do on a bicycle.'

Communions were held twice a year in all parishes and lasted for five days, from Thursday until the following Monday. They were held at different times in all the parishes, and this gave an opportunity to the other parishes to join in, and indeed they did, for they flocked in hundreds from all parts of the island to the communion centre. In the old days, it was customary to remain for the full period. Every available corner of the household was used for sleeping, and in many cases the overflow slept on straw in the barns. There was strong competition and rivalry as to who would have the most visitors. Nobody was turned away and the lodging was free. Anything up to twenty visitors was not uncommon. There was some strain, of course, on the food supply and utensils, but potatoes and fish were plentiful at that time and that was the backbone of the meal.

Communions are still regularly held in the isles but the old ways have changed. Not so many people go now and they travel back and fore in buses and cars. They return home the same night. Streams of these buses could be seen on the last day of the communion as they returned home. I have seen as many as twenty buses in one long line returning, and it was pleasant to listen to the mournful singing of psalms from the people as it passed through the village on a quiet autumn evening.

In the ceilidh house a certain amount of leg-pulling went on between the religious folk and the others. During a meal on one of these occasions one of the wags asked, after the man of the house said a long grace before his meal, 'Do you think, Torquil, that God heard your grace?' 'Every word of it,' replied Torquil reverently. 'Oh well,' said Donald, as he rose to go, 'I am sure he enjoyed it and had a good laugh to himself.'

Another chap just happened to be sitting down to a meal when the village elder appeared in the doorway. Angus had not been in the habit of saying grace and knew his grace was a bit rusty. So partly to get over the difficulty, the elder was begged to sit and join them. Angus knew well that the honour of saying grace would fall to the elder and thus he himself would be able to escape his predicament. But it did not turn out according to plan. The elder refused out and out to have anything to eat, and so Angus was forced to face the ordeal with his rusty grace. He did not want to disgrace his household in the eyes of a pillar of the church, so he tried to hide his inability by mumbling in a monotone as he drew his hand reverently backwards and forwards across his face. When he was finished, the elder remarked that he had not heard a single word of his grace. 'That may be so,' answered Angus, 'but it was not with you I was doing business.'

I have listened spellbound to the delivery of some of these old, uneducated and untravelled crofters on *la na ceist* (the day of questions) during communion. The logical reasoning, the flow of language and the humble and earnest way in which they approached it were a pleasure and a delight to the ear.

10

THE WATER OF LIFE

The Gaelic name for whisky is *uisge beatha*, or water of life. It has certainly played an important part in Highland life. During my youth most Highland folk took it, but not in the quantities described by some modern writers. Every old *cailleach* and *bodach* would take a dram, indeed some would say, 'It is my friend that would give it to me'. It was the wonderful elixir that brought joy to one's heart and a smile to one's face.

Illicit distilling as practised in the old days is gone, and I doubt if there is a single still in the isles today. There were times, however, when I thought there were. A friend always insisted on giving me a dram every New Year morning, and he always asked the same question when I had sampled it: 'What do you think of it?' I always suspected that it had never crossed the Minch. Whisky can be made from practically anything, and heather, I am told, makes excellent whisky.

I knew one old chap who had spent most of his life in the Canadian bush, and who came back, as many did, to spend his last days in the isles. Whenever he felt in the mood for a dram, he would collect all the old potato peelings, overripe fruit, etc., put the mixture in a pot over the fire and let it steam. He covered the top of the pot with a bit of old blanket instead of a lid. Occasionally he would lift the blanket off and wring it over a cup. It did not take very long until he had a glass of pure raw alcohol; it was not pleasant to drink but Callum had a throat like leather and didn't seem to notice any difference.

At other times, he would use a kettle and employ a cold slate to catch the steam coming from the spout. The steam condensed on contact with the cold slate, and drop by drop he would fill up his glass.

Beer was made by many crofters, and potent stuff it was! The old crofter whom I saw brewing his own lived in the old type of house with the fire in the middle of the floor, the cattle in the far end and the sleeping quarters in the upper end. The floor was of clay throughout the house.

He had a heap of barley in the upper end in the middle of the floor with a bit of tarpaulin spread underneath. Water was poured occasionally on the grain to keep it moist. There would be about two bushels of grain in the heap, and it was left there until the grain sprouted. Fermentation set in then, and the wash taken off it was the beer. It was a long, laborious job. Winter was the favourite time for doing it, and many crofters kept a supply of it for the spring time when the croft work began.

On ploughing day and the day for taking home the peats, a dram was always served at all the meals. On rent days and market days, which involved a visit to the town, most crofters came home in jovial mood, and there was always a wee drappie for the household. These were, of course, red letter days, and perhaps for the rest of the year many did not see it at all. Seldom were excesses to be seen except when the young lads went to town quarterly to draw the militia or R.N.R. retainer.

There was usually some village rivalry which often ended in blows. These fights were always fair, and if one fell, the other waited until he was set for the fight again and no blows were struck except with the fists.

To the stranger, drinking always appeared excessive in the town of Stornoway. There are reasons for this. First, the facilities for entertainment were too few and second, the improvement in roads and bus services to the various villages threw an extra burden on the limited entertainment. The population of the town was five thousand but there were twenty-four thousand people living in the rural districts who were able to travel to town on the Saturday night, if they wished. There were only nine or ten licensed premises in town and they had to provide the requirements of the rest of the population since there were no licences on the island outside the town.

The town went dry at one time under the Temperance or Licensing Act. All the hotels were closed to retail drinks, but strangely enough, they still had a wholesale licence and could sell a minimum of four and a half gallons of beer. The result was that small clubs were formed to purchase four and a half gallons. Each club had its own drum or can and a supply of tin mugs. Perhaps this is what gave some visitors the impression that it was being drunk by the pailful. The can, when filled, was taken down to a quiet corner on the pier or a secluded spot among the herring barrels where the beer was shared out.

The amount of beer consumed in a dry area was alarming, as was shown by the dozens of hogsheads awaiting shipment each week on the pier—indeed an oasis in the desert! Less liquor was drunk, yet the four and a half business was unsightly and an eyesore to the community. Naturally, the town went 'wet' again at a later poll and the only difference was that they drank inside instead of outside.

When I was young there were several shebeens in the town, and one woman in my own village served a term in jail for shebeening. There were certain crimes which left no blot on a Highlander's character: taking a salmon out of the burn, a deer off the hill, and distilling or shebeening. When the jailer's wife asked her, 'What sent you in here?', old Katie, who had little English, replied, 'John Barleycorn, a ghraidh' (John Barleycorn, my dear).

One local worthy who used to do odd jobs about the town got an occasional dram during his rounds. He was not really addicted to drink but his wife hated its very name. One day, Coinneach (Kenneth) came home having had one or two. His wife, of course, smelled it and Coinneach got the usual tirade. She went on and on and on. Like the guest in the Ancient Mariner, he had no choice but to listen while she held him with her clattering tongue. Coinneach waited patiently until she had exhausted herself, and then remarked, 'I can't understand it at all, Peggy. It puzzles me very much. I cannot fathom it at all'. 'Can't fathom what?' she rapped. To her great astonishment Coinneach replied, 'The glass I take, it is into your head it goes'.

A resident in my own district was asked by the innkeeper as he was passing if he would give him a turn with a cask he was putting on the gantry. 'Indeed, it is myself that will,' he replied. 'Many a good turn it has given me.'

On New Year's Eve or immediately after midnight it was the custom for young men to first foot their friends and neighbours. This meant practically everybody in the village. One seldom managed to complete the whole round. The usual toasts were drunk in each house, the health of relatives and friends. The usual term or toast in Gaelic is 'slaint' or 'slainte mhath' or 'slainte mhor', meaning health, good health or big health. Sometimes there were additions to these terms like, 'a h-uile la a chi is nach fhaic' (every day I see you and don't see you). A dram was taken first out of the visitor's bottle and then one out of the host's. When this was repeated in several houses, the effects were soon showing and the scheduled programme had to be abandoned.

The young men always tried to make the old men tipsy. One such old man, Murchadh Thormaid, had so many visitors that he had to be put to bed. Next morning, one of the men called to see Murchadh in order to give him a 'livener', but Murdo was adamant. He was sitting up in bed with a red handkerchief with white spots round his head and looking like a retired pirate. 'Come on, Murdo, a wee one will put you right.' Murdo looked at the bottle and moaned, holding his head with both hands, 'Out of my sight with it, out of my sight with it, even if it was empty, out of my sight with it'. Murdo had over-celebrated and that was him off it at least until time had healed the memory.

One crofter, when drawing the old-fashioned cork out with a corkscrew, was heard to remark when he heard the 'gog' of the drawn cork, 'There's a gog for you, and not the gog of the moor hen'.

The water of life has played an important part in Highland life, especially at feasts and weddings, and as the Gaelic proverb says, 'Cha bhith a chuirm na cuirm mar a bith e roimpe agus as a deigh' (A feast is no feast unless it, whisky, is served before and after it).

II

COURTSHIP

As a rule, couples did not get married in the isles at such an early age as they tended to do in the south. Generally, the courtship was a long one and as secret as possible. In fact, the main aim was that nobody should know or even suspect that a wedding was about to take place until the event was publicly announced. To the stranger this might appear well-nigh impossible in a community where everybody knew one another and where they went daily in and out of one another's houses. Sometimes suspicions were aroused where an extra spring cleaning was given to the house or where a room was repapered when it had been done a short time before. Nevertheless, in most cases, it was a great secret until the *reiteach* (espousal) was announced.

Courting in the isles was not done in public and couples did not walk out together. The custom of bundling was common in days gone by and indeed lingered on in some areas. The introduction of the white house and then electric light probably dealt the fatal blow. The white house was not suited for the custom because bedrooms were upstairs and the main door was barred and locked unless a 'fifth columnist' had unlocked the doors before going to bed. But there were ways and means of getting over the locked door problem, as was proved in some cases.

In this particular village, the black house had practically disappeared, but nevertheless, the bundling went on. The young men cycled from the neighbouring village after bedtime. They would find the ladder at the back of the byre or barn, place it against the bedroom window, and with the connivance of his ladylove, get admission this way. He left as usual before dawn, replaced the ladder behind the barn and cycled quietly home.

One winter's night, however, the cycling lovers had a rude awakening. It was a beautiful night when the ladders were scaled, but there were six to eight feet of snow on the ground when it was time to come down. The result was that the ladder could not be removed and the bicycles could not be found. Worse was to come, as the standing ladders below the windows of many young girls in the village were evidence that they all had boy friends; and further, when the thaw set in, the handlebars of one bicycle after another appeared, and it also became known who each boy friend was.

Bundling was the custom of visiting one's fiancée after bed time and staying with her all night. In the eyes of some, the custom appeared strange and probably even immoral, but I would assure these people that cases of indecency were more or less unknown and that the code of honour was very high. Paradoxically, the more that so-called civilisation infiltrated into the isles, the more the code of honour degenerated.

Conditions in the isles favoured the custom of bundling. The door of the black house was never bolted or locked. Many of the doors had no lock of any kind. It was not needed and the people knew they could trust one another in all things. Never have I known of any house being entered in order to steal.

The would-be suitor arrived at his tryst shortly after midnight, having made his way thither in the shade of walls and peatstacks to hide himself from the prying eyes of the younger or curious lads who made it their business to know who so and so was courting. If there was a bright moon, the lover stayed at home or avoided the road by cutting through the crofts. On arrival he silently lifted the latch in case the *bodach* (old man) or *cailleach* (old woman) who were sleeping in the *culaist* (best room) would hear him. He also had to beware of, and even sometime silence, a growling dog. Dogs, however, were so used to noises of all kinds from cows, sheep and fowl that it was seldom they paid any attention.

When the wooer got inside, he made sure he could not be followed, by jamming the spade or the graip which were always kept behind the *tallan* (partition) against the door. If it was a first visit and the reception was cold, then it was obvious he was not wanted or that the young lady had a boy friend already. There was nothing for it but to make his exit as silently as he made his entrance. If the door was barred on his arrival, he knew immediately that the lady was otherwise engaged. If the reception was friendly, he was permitted to take his boots off and stretch himself on top of the bed. The room was never really cold and a smooring peat or two in the ashes kept the fire alive.

One young man who was courting a girl in a Lewis village joined the forces during the First World War. He was serving in a Highland regiment on the Balkan front when word was received from the War Office that he was missing, presumed killed. A wake was held at his home just the same as if the body were there. However, the war came to an end and one day John arrived back home. He had been a prisoner-of-war in the Balkans and had had no means of letting his people at home know. He thoroughly enjoyed the story of the wake and heard about all the people who had gathered to mourn his loss. His fiancée, however, had not attended the wake, probably because of her great distress. When this became known to John, he did not continue the courtship, and when asked what had happened between himself and Mairi, replied, 'Well, if she did not think it worth while to come to my wake, then I have no further use for her'.

During the winter, when no croft work or peats had to be attended to, life in the isles could be very pleasant, and apart from the feeding and milking of the animals, and perhaps a little fishing, there was little to do except pass the time ceilidhing. Time meant very little then and the people were late in going to bed and late in rising. Schools did not assemble until ten o'clock.

Even when summer time was introduced, few people paid the slightest attention to it. They kept God's time and were not going to change it for any Act of Parliament. They were philosophical about it. As one old fellow said, 'If everything was as plentiful as time, we would be well off. Look at the amount of it that is gone and the amount that is to come. The Almighty was lavish with time; it is unlimited'. There was no bus or train to catch and no timetable to work to. One old lady, on being asked if she had changed the clock to the new time, replied, 'No, I am not going to touch it. My clock is an old clock and would not stand the new time'. And so with the custom of bundling, there was no factory whistle blowing at eight o'clock in the morning, and the young lads could stay in bed all the following day if they wished.

12

HALLOWE'EN

Only two of the ancient Celtic festivals survive in the isles, Hallowe'en and Hogmanay or *calluinn*. They have both lost all their original significance, but traces of the original can be detected.

During my youth, at the turn of the century, the children clubbed together according to their ages and saved up all their pennies for weeks before Hallowe'en in order to provide the apples and nuts required for the occasion. The location of the party was kept a secret, and on Hallowe'en night a black shawl was placed over the window so that the house looked unoccupied.

There were reasons for this great secrecy, because if the other groups discovered where we were holding our party, all sorts of tricks would be played on us. It was so easy to climb on to the roof of a thatched cottage and throw a peat down the chimney if there was one. If the soup or potatoes were on the fire, the contents were usually tainted by the shower of soot that came down with the peat.

On the table was an ashet piled up like a volcano with mashed potatoes. Each boy had a bowl of milk and a spoon in front of him. Spoons were not so plentiful then and had to be gathered from the nearby houses. Spoonful after spoonful of the potatoes was taken, dipped in the milk and eaten. It was a glorious feast, and the good lady had told us that the one who could eat the most of the potatoes and milk would get that extra apple or slice of bread with jam. Jam, of course, was a luxury in those days.

Hallowe'en

And so we dug into the steaming volcano until it was extinct and not a crumb left on the ashet, with the result that few of us had any room left for the extra luxuries.

The apples and nuts were afterwards shared out equally. I do remember one party where we decided to 'dook' for the apples. A huge wooden washing tub with about a foot of water in it was placed in the middle of the floor. One by one we took our turn at the dooking, and it became obvious that it was paying off for one of the boys very well. 'Braxy', who was a big powerful fellow for his age, had a few apples in his pockets before we were able to get even one. He had the courage to plunge his head right down and jam the apple against the bottom of the tub. It was becoming alarmingly clear that there would not be enough apples to go round, and so the cry went up, 'Share the apples, share the apples!' All the apples were returned and an equal share was given to each one.

The apples were peeled with a knife and everyone tried to get the peel off in one long piece. It was then thrown over the shoulder, and whatever initial it formed on the floor, that was to be the initial of your future husband or wife. We laid the nuts on a glowing peat ember, and whichever one cracked or jumped first, that would be the first one to be married. If the nuts jumped together, then these two would surely marry each other!

Then came the time for fortune telling. We filled our mouths with water and ran from one house to another, making a humming noise at each window until some girl looked out. That one was to be your future wife. One old unmarried lady always took us in to tell our fortunes. She would crack an egg for us and let the albumen spread itself in fantastic shapes in a tumblerful of water. The most wonderful scenes would appear in the water and she proceeded to interpret them all. We stood open-mouthed listening to it all, and we believed it, and probably the strong Celtic imagination helped us to see it. I was to be a sailor, for there was the lighthouse standing at the harbour mouth and in the background was a full-rigged ship with her white sails crowding. Another boy was to be a shepherd or a farmer for we saw the flock of sheep quite plainly being driven along the road with the farmer and his dog behind him. And so it went on until all our futures were told.

After midnight, the boys prowled around looking for innocent mischief or jokes to play on various people. The boys, of course, had their favourites, those who were nice and kind to them, and they also remembered those who had ill-treated them. They were always the victims of the ploys.

Donnachadh Ruadh vowed that no cabbages would be taken from his garden; he would see to that. He told the boys he was going to sit all night behind the corn stack with his gun and that he would shoot the first one he saw tampering with his garden. And he did sit there, but long before dark the boys, including his own son, tied a string to some of the cabbages and carried the line over the garden wall. Donnachadh waited patiently and was in fact wearying that nothing was happening. Then he saw cabbage after cabbage leave its allotted place in the garden and hop over the wall. He retired to the house as quickly as he could, white as a sheet, and told his wife that devils like those which had entered the Gadarene swine had entered his cabbages and that they were dancing all over the place.

There was one crofter who was very hard on boys, and one Hallowe'en they shifted his peatstack to the other side of the road. They started after midnight with several creels and by dawn had the stack on the other side. We used to hollow out the stalk of a cabbage, fill it up with peat fibre and blow the smoke through the keyhole to give the impression that the house was on fire. Practically every thatched house had the chimney blocked with a *sgrath* (divot) placed on the top.

If any carts were left outside, they would be found in the

morning a mile or two away. But Tormod Iain was puzzled how they moved his cart into his own barn (and him after padlocking the wheels to the shafts). The boys removed the axle pins, took the wheels off and slid the chain over the ends of the shafts. Then willing hands placed the cart on edge and lifted it through the barn door. The wheels were then replaced the same way and the axle pins put in. Tormod never found out how it was done.

Perhaps the cruellest of the ploys was when Ishbel's cow was removed and Jockan's horse tied up in the byre in its place. Ishbel was getting old and blind but could feel her way around quite well. When milking time came round, poor Ishbel took her little stool and sat under the pony and tried to milk it!

La Calluinn (Hogmanay) was originally on the twelfth of January, old New Year's Day. The old people used to say there was an hour extra on the day on Calluinn day. The ploy was not the same on Hogmanay as on Hallowe'en. Groups of boys would gather together and go from door to door *bualadh na Calluinn*. One boy carried a sheepskin over his back and two others repeated the *duan* or rant. One kept on repeating Ho vi ri o, while the other answered with a line of the rant: Ho vi ri o, We have come here tonight, Ho vi ri o, to remind you of the Calluinn; Ho vi ri o, We did not need to do so, Ho vi ri o. It was there from the days of my grandfather; Ho vi ri o, Good housewife, arise; Ho vi ri o, and go up and get the bannock; we take the bread without butter and the butter without bread, ending with a blessing on the house and all who are in it.

On concluding the rant, we would be invited inside, when the lad with the sheepskin circled the fire three times sunwise. At the same time, blow after blow was heaped on the skin with the tongs or any other handy weapon, as he passed around. Then the bag the children carried, usually a pillowcase, was opened and the housewife's contribution put in.

13

FUN AND GAMES

The winters were always long in the isles. Our high latitude gave us a long winter and a short summer. Lamps were lit in midwinter about four o'clock in the afternoon and I often pitied the hens which roosted about four o'clock and were on the perch until nine o'clock the following morning. The longest night of the year in December was called 'Oidhche na seachd suipeirean' (the night of the seven suppers), probably because of the extra meals required during the long night.

Children had little or nothing to do during these long nights apart from accompanying their mothers to the byre to help with the feeding and milking of the cattle. Otherwise they went ceilidhing to a near neighbour's house which had children of the same age. We were really so scared of the supernatural that we were afraid to go too far from our own home. So many stories had been heard of a light seen here or a ghost there that the whole village seemed haunted.

Toys were more or less unknown except perhaps a doll for the wee one. The doll, as a rule, was the *sguab mhuran* (brush of bent grass) with granny's small plaid wrapped around it. The cradle was the small stool turned upside down. The stool also served as a horse or a boat for the wee boy during the day. The tongs were stuck through the hole on the top as a mast and any handy garment used as a sail. Good and bad weather was encountered, and I have watched the boat being wrecked and the wee lad swimming for his life to the shore.

Fun and Games

The favourite nights for inside games were Tuesdays and Thursdays when the prayer meetings were held in the village. Cards were forbidden as they were the work of the devil, but later on, I have seen cards being played in many houses. The most popular game was Catching the Ten, but I have seen my father and some other old sailors playing Euchre. They taught us the game, but I have never seen it played since.

When the village hall was erected, whist drives were regularly held. One young woman who was getting ready for one of these whists was asked by her mother where she was going. 'To a whist drive in the hall,' replied the girl. 'What is a whist drive?' she asked. 'Oh,' answered the girl, evading the truth, 'we play games and have a cup of tea.' 'That is not so bad,' replied her mother, 'I don't mind as long as you do not play cards there.'

During the late autumn when the harvest moon was on, we played hide and seek among the corn stooks. Half the team would be in the den while the other half went out to hide. The idea was for those in hiding to get back to the den without being caught. When they were all caught, the other side went out to hide.

The hunter's moon was called *geallach cul nan cnuic* or 'the moon of the backs of the hills'. The moon had its least altitude then and the deer could be plainly seen silhouetted against it.

A popular game was the Cock and the Hen. The cock and the hen stood facing each other. The hen had all her chickens behind her, each one hanging on to the tail of the other's jacket or jersey. The following conversation took place in Gaelic:

Hen   What do you want?
Cock   A needle.
Hen   What is the needle for?

Cock   To sew a bag.
Hen   What is the bag for?
Cock   For peats.
Hen   What are the peats for?
Cock   To make a fire.
Hen   What is the fire for?
Cock   For a pot.
Hen   What is the pot for?
Cock   For water.
Hen   What is the water for?
Cock   To boil one of your chickens.
Hen   Gog, gog. You won't get them.
Cock   Gog, gog. I will.

Most of our games had penalties. Here is one popular knife game which we played while we were herding. You took the open knife in your hand, put the point to each finger in turn and stabbed it into the ground. The same thing was repeated with the knife in the left hand. Next, it was laid open on the closed fist, first with the blade towards you and then with the blade away from you. With a twist of the wrist it had to be stuck into the ground from both positions. Finally, the tip of the knife was put in the ground and it was somersaulted along the ground. If it stuck in the ground, you were out. You then had the privilege of sticking the blade in the ground from a standing position as deeply as you could, and were allowed to cut a turf of that depth of blade, that width and that length.

The last man in took the penalty. He had to stand ten paces away with his back towards us, bend down and touch his toes. All the boys who were in the game were allowed to throw the turf at his posterior. Few missed the target as they were all expert at throwing. The soft turf never did much damage even when a bull was scored and it was good fun. This accuracy in stone throwing served the nation well later during the great war of 1914, when the Mills bomb was much in use. It is a known fact that Highland boys were specially picked for this job because of their accuracy and length of throw.

Games seem naturally to follow seasons, and children turn to the seasonal as instinctively as the cuckoo comes in the summer. The bane of the mothers of the isles was the button season. A quiet sheltered spot was chosen where the ground could be softened by patting and a *spid* or small twig stuck in the soft patch. It was like the modern game of pitch and toss or quoits, except that buttons were used as pitchers. The ideal pitcher was a heavy iron button. Small buttons such as vest buttons were not accepted. Some boys introduced large oilskin buttons as pitchers but they were also rejected.

The stance was about eight feet from the *spid* or pin and you had to throw your pitcher as near to it as you could. If you were not satisfied with your throw you could have two more. Blowing through the button was considered to be very lucky, so each boy faithfully blew through before throwing. When all had exhausted their chances, the one nearest the pin collected all the buttons, cupped them in his two hands, shook them well, blew on them and finally threw them in the air. All the buttons lying face up were his. The one who was second repeated the same process with the remaining buttons, and so on until all the buttons were won. Pitchers were then exchanged for another button and a new game started.

Like all gamblers we played on until no buttons were left. Obviously, parents did not approve of this game, for like the man who puts his shirt on a horse, we often went home holding up our trousers or with a bit of string round the waist. Button after button was cut off as the game went on, and like gambling, it went further and further. Many a *cailleach* found her husband's best Sunday trousers hanging on the clothes line buttonless. Mention of it could be heard in the ceilidh house, 'Na plaighean, cha do dh'fhag iad putan ann am briogais Iain' (The plague on them, they did not leave a button in John's trousers).

But of all our fun and games, priority number one was sailing model boats. Every boy had one, not one bought in a shop with beautiful white sails, but a home-made one. A bit of three-by-two timber with a piece of hoop iron to serve as a keel was fine. We had a choice of several lochs but the favourite one was Loch na Barrachs at Holm. This had sea water in it and was clear of grass and moss round the edge. *Faire, faire*! How many generations of Sandwick and Holm boys sailed their boats on that loch and 'where are those dreamers now?'

All our boats were the *Zulu* type, perpendicular stem and sloping stern. Sometimes the steering was done by giving a small turn to the iron hoop which served as a keel, and at times we had a proper rudder. Three holes were made in the stern of the boat with a red-hot knitting wire and three more opposite these in the rudder. The rudder was then tied tightly on with string.

Few if any of the boats had a jib. We didn't know much about that type, but we could do anything with the lug sail. Hemp thread was used as halyards and the eyelets of old boots as blocks. The great idea was to get them to go as close to the wind as possible, and with the lug sail carried well aft you could get them to go into the very eye of the wind. We took our type from the fishing boats which were all lug-rigged. These fishing boats were wonderful to sail and none of them was known to capsize. If too much sail was carried, the mast would go by the stump before the boat would go over.

Sometimes we had difficulty in getting sails, so much so that 'Brown' cut one out of his mother's shirt which he found bleaching on the green. She was quite distressed about it but we never told what had happened. Shirts were just not so plentiful as they arc today, and many people wore flour-bag shirts with the colours as far as possible bleached out of them. I remember one crofter who had a flour bag back to his vest; it read FANCY BRAND, Roller Process, 112 lbs. in red letters.

Two old fishing boats were lying derelict for years on the edge of the loch, and if the weather was very cold we used them as shelter to watch the tacking from one side of the loch to the other. We did not wear boots. We tucked our trousers over our thighs, and waded out to catch the boats and return them on the next tack across the loch. This went on until dusk chased us home, cold, wet and happy. What a boys' paradise!

We did not get much snow and frost in winter; the weather was, as a rule, wet and windy but very mild. One exceptional snowstorm completely covered up some of the thatched houses. Men were walking on top of Alasdair Enag's house trying to locate its exact spot, when Alasdair himself, wondering that dawn was not arriving, pushed a long bamboo fishing rod up through the thatch and snow. It took many men half the day to dig a passage through to his door.

If snow was on the ground we spent the time catching birds, particularly the grey linnet. The linnet is a lovely singer and we could always sell them. A hoop covered with herring net was used. The hoop was placed in a slanting position with a stick to support it. Oat seed and crumbs were placed under it, and whenever the birds went underneath, the stick was pulled and the hoop fell flat. Only the linnets were kept; the starlings, sparrows and blackbirds were immediately set free. The poor linnet, whose only crime was that it could sing, was sentenced to penal servitude for life.

Another method but not so effective was the *buthach*. This was a peat to which many nooses of horse's hair had been attached and pinned down with match sticks. Oat seed and crumbs of bread were spread on the peat. It was then placed on top of a corn stack or any place frequented by the birds. Their legs got entangled in the nooses and they couldn't fly away.

Putting the stone was practised most evenings in the summertime. Even the adults tried their hand at this. But *La Caluinn* (January 12th) was the great day. The inter-village shinty game was on that day. Any number could play on each side and nobody had a shinty stick of the kind we see today. There was no growing timber in Lewis in those days, so all the *camans* were cut from the whin bush. The *caman* or club was from eighteen inches to two feet long and was used mainly with the one hand. I cannot remember all the rules, but you could not turn round and face the same way as your opponent when tackling. You then heard the shout of 'Seas do chulag' (Stand your ground properly).

A mark at each end of the field indicated the goal. The ball had not to be driven between two posts but beyond a mark. When that happened, everybody shouted 'Hilo!' In the previous generation they even had to make their own ball. In those days, most of the boots had rubber soles. All the discarded boots were collected and the rubber fashioned into a ball with the red hot tongs. One had to be careful not to toast one's toes too near the fire, or a stream of melted rubber was left on the hearth and the rest of the company held their noses. Rubber, however, had its advantages. Repairs were easily executed; if a crack or hole appeared on the sole, you just ran the hot tongs along it and the crack was sealed up.

One mischievous practice was to sprinkle a spadeful of live ashes in the dark passage leading into the kitchen.

Fun and Games

Most people went barefoot in the summer weather, and when they trampled on the hot cinders, the boys who were watching the fun got a great kick out of the exclamation, 'foiteag, foiteag' as the victim ran to rub her soles. Some of the soles were so hard that even hot cinders did not affect them. Domhnull Ossian used to say he could run barefoot as fast on the Sgeir Mhor (the long rock) as he would in the meal cist.

14

FROM CRUISIE TO ELECTRIC

Slowly but surely, the electric power provided by the Hydro Electric Board spread through the isles, until eventually the whole island was served.

The last of the *cruisgeans* or cruisies disappeared during the last half of the nineteenth century; electric light arrived during the last half of the twentieth. Thus, for a hundred years, the paraffin lamp in all its variations remained the only source of lighting.

I had never actually seen the cruisie in use in my own native village, but there were parts of the island where it was still in use. It was a very primitive form of lighting and seems to have been used in some form or other all over the world. It consisted of a shallow metal saucer-like container filled with oil. A rag or piece of string served as a wick, one end of which was in the oil, and the other, which hung over the lip of the saucer, gave the flame. Like many other early inventions, it was crude and not any more effective than an ordinary candle. In the olden days, the wick was made from the inner pith of rushes which grew profusely in any damp meadow land. The outer skin of the rushes was removed and the porous nature of the inner stem provided the capillary attraction which drew the oil along its length.

The oil was not bought. It was all made from fish or animal liver. Seal was fairly common and yielded very valuable oil which had medicinal qualities as well. People drank it in cold weather and used it for burns and wounds. The main source of oil supplies was fish liver. There was an ample supply of fish; in fact, in many cases it was left to rot on the shore after the liver had been extracted. Even long after markets were found, flat fishes like turbot, halibut, roker, skate and flounders could not then be transported. These fishes could not be salted and dried successfully and had to be used immediately while fresh. It was common for the fishermen to use the halibut and roker as skids to drag their boats up on the beach.

Skate particularly could not be salted, and strangely enough, did not turn maggoty like the other fish. It turned sour, and many people preferred to use it when in that condition. Only the two wings were used, the head and abdomen, which comprise most of the fish, being thrown away. The wings were hung on a nail in the wall to dry in the sun for several days, or wrapped up in a cloth and buried for a few days. The fish by that time took on a reddish bacon-like appearance. It was then in prime condition. It smelled like raw ammonia, and I can vouch for its qualities to give instant relief to the sufferer from nasal catarrh or bronchial congestion. It just took one's breath away and the nose and throat felt as if they were one large open cavity.

Most houses had paraffin lamps during my youth, but the next improvement after the cruisie was *lampa cheard* or the tinker's lamp. The tinkers were tinsmiths and went from door to door selling tinware of all kinds. The origin of the tinsmithing trade among the tinkers was interesting. After the Peninsular War and the downfall of Napoleon at Waterloo, Highland and Scottish regiments were disbanded. Many of the troops were discharged, and as there were no pensions, a grateful government taught them the tinsmith trade, sending them round the country to earn their bread and butter the best way they could. They had no homes and thus became vagrants wandering from place to place.

Peat Fire Memories

The tinker's lamp was conical in shape with the top of the cone cut off about an inch from the top. The diameter of the base was about four inches. A small thin disc about the size of a penny carried through its centre a narrow funnel which contained the wick. It was a great improvement on the cruisie as it did away with all the melting of fish liver and its accompanying unpleasant smell, but then it was much more dangerous in a thatched house, and the smell was still there, only that it was different. In fact, in some respects the smell was worse. If any meat or particularly bread was in the same room, it invariably smelled and tasted of paraffin. It was amazing how seldom thatched houses caught fire. Sparks could be seen rising to the well-sooted thatch but never seemed to do any damage.

The tinker's lamp lost its honoured position when the paraffin globe or chimney lamp appeared. It was relegated to the barn or byre where it served a very useful purpose while the cattle were being fed or milked. In fact, it was better for that purpose than any of its successors.

The globe lamp was the next step forward. It was cleaner to work with and lessened the number of *cailleachan suich* (sooty ladies) which floated around when the tinker's lamp was well under steam, as it were. The lighting was much better though more costly owing to the extra expense of paraffin globes. Globes were selling at threepence each and paraffin was three halfpence a bottle, six bottles to the gallon. There was always a wee shop or two which sold the strange combination of bread and paraffin.

Most people used the type of lamp with the round corrugated reflector on the back. It stood on the mantle-piece or the dresser, or hung from a nail in the wall. The container held about a pint of oil. The lamp had to be attended to daily by removing the crust which formed on the wick, filling the container and cleaning the globe. If the wick crust was not removed, the lamp gave poor light, the flame flickered up and down, blackened the globe and sometimes broke it.

Globes were very fragile and great care was needed when cleaning them. When on the lamp, the globe got very hot and the least drop of water or sudden cold draught from the door cracked the glass and the top would fall off. This, of course, happened fairly often, but it was not then discarded. A round bit of paper was fixed on for a top and many globes have stood service in this way, although the light was not so good. If any water got into the oil, the light sputtered up and down.

The lamp served other purposes as well as lighting. Blotting paper was not so common then, and many of the old folk found the top of the globe a very convenient place to dry their letters, written with an ink pen. Evidence of this was to be seen by the recipient when a singed circular patch appeared in the middle of the page where it had been left that second too long over the top of the globe. There were many varieties of the paraffin lamp; some were for hanging on the wall, some sat on the dresser and others could be hung from the ceiling.

Later, the *lampa mhor* or big lamp appeared. It had two globes, one which acted as a chimney and the other which fitted outside the chimney. It was for decorative purposes and had an attractive floral design. This type had a double wick and gave double the lighting. It always sat on the table in the *seomair* or best room and was only used for special occasions, these being mainly wakes, funerals and weddings. If you did not have one of your own for these occasions, you borrowed your neighbour's and also the glass water jug which always stood beside the bible on the crimson table cloth. Neighbours were very kind on these occasions and lent their chairs and anything that was necessary.

Crofters often denied themselves the bare necessities in order to get something nice for 'the room' and then rarely used it. I knew of many attractive rooms in my own native village that were never used from one year's end to the other. One progressive lady I knew used to refer to it as 'the mortuary'!

Inevitably came the turn of the *lampa mhor* to go the way of its predecessors—the incandescent had arrived. This was the mantle type of lamp, and it was such an improvement on all the others that it soon established itself in practically every home in the isles. It was a little more troublesome than the other but it gave an excellent, bright white light which heated the room as well. They were, of course, more expensive in mantles and generators. The strain on the eyes when reading was reduced, and one could now read comfortably in any part of the room, but with the old lamp one had to be right up against it. If old Dan had lived longer, he would have appreciated the new light. Dan was one of the few who always got a weekly paper and could be seen at night with two pairs of glasses on, sitting as near as possible to the lamp, reading his paper. Dan wore two pairs of glasses because the left eye glass was missing in one pair and the right in the other.

Then the electric power arrived with all its amenities: no more looking for matches, or blowing at a dying peat ember when you arrived home after a day on the moor, at the peats or the croft, trying to ignite a paper in order to light the lamp, no more nasty smell of paraffin or toasting of oat bannocks by the fire, and no more cursing of wireless sets when the battery conked out in the middle of the Gaelic programme. All wireless sets in the isles were battery sets.

An old lady asked her next-door neighbour during the war if there was anything fresh on the wireless. 'No,' he replied, 'the accumulator is down.' 'Dear me, dear me, another one,' she sobbed. 'Was there a big loss of life?'

It was a great boon to the crofter to press a button at his barn or byre door and find the place beautifully lit up instead of fumbling with matches or carrying a glowing peat in order to light the tinker's lamp. It was reported from one of the villages that the collector who called to read the meter was surprised how little current was used in a certain house during the quarter, but he was told that they only used 'the electric' while they were getting the lamps ready!

There is no doubt that electric power revolutionised life in the isles. It dealt the death blow to many bad customs and unfortunately to many good ones. The ceilidh house as we knew it is gone. Modern progress and real ceilidhs do not go together. You have to knock at most doors now and wait for the invitation to come in. There are carpets on the floor and cushions on the chairs, and you cannot smoke volumes of thick, black tobacco and spit accurately from a distance into the fire. The ceilidh now is in a hall, and that in a way is a good thing, but there will be no peat reek, no sooty *caber*, no drink of pure spring water from the tinker's jug, no steady thump of the flail behind the *tallan* and no mellow lowing of cattle at milking time. These conditions were essential for a real ceilidh.

A new era had crept in. It brought with it many improvements, but it has swept away many things which the older generations cherished and held dear, something that money cannot buy—the traditional *ceud mile failte* of a kind and hospitable people. Civilisation, so called, had reached the isles and commercialism and distrust along with it. I wonder whether it might not have been better to have 'am bonnach beag agus am beannachd no am bonnach more agus am mollachd' (the small bannock and the blessing, than the big one and the curse).

15

Flotsam

The motto of the town of Stornoway is 'God's Providence is our Inheritance', because the town is, or was, dependent on the produce of the sea. But God's providence manifests itself in many ways, and particularly by the flotsam washed up after severe winter gales. How much the isles depended on this in the past can be gathered from the fact that libations of liquor used to be poured into the sea in Lewis to the god Shonny as a gesture of thanks for these benefits.

It is not so very long ago since wrecks and flotsam were regularly prayed for in the isles. Little or no thought was given to the loss of property. The wreck was looked upon by the islesmen as a god-sent gift to alleviate their poverty. The lives of sailors were, however, sacred in the isles, and in this there was a remarkable contrast with the attitude in the south of England, where it is on record that it was not proper to save the life of a stricken sailor. Providence meant him to drown, and so he was pushed back into the sea.

In my own native village, the beach was divided up into portions according as the crofts touched the shore. Nobody dared lay hands on anything that came ashore on another person's portion. Winter seaweed, or *feamainn thilgte*, was very valuable, and each person gathered regularly the seaweed thrown up on his part of the shore. Much, of course, depended on the direction of the prevailing wind as to where the seaweed gathered, but, over the whole winter, nature and the elements saw to a fair distribution over the beach generally. Sometimes the seaweed was spread on the croft as winter manure, and sometimes it was laid in the midden or compost heap.

In the springtime, when the big tides were on, the crofters went out to the sunken reefs immediately after the tide had left them. A bit of an old trawl was spread out on the reefs and rapidly filled up with seaweed. When the tide turned, the net was gathered round the heap, firmly secured with ropes and left until the tide would lift it. A fair quantity of bladder wrack had to be included in the *maois*, or heap, in order to give it buoyancy, otherwise it would not float. When the tide was full in, a boat went out to secure the seaweed and pull it to the beach. It was a heavy tow, as the heap was usually about eight feet in diameter, six or seven feet deep and floated with only the surface showing.

Four oars were needed on the boat for this job and each pull only gave about a yard of progress. However, in time it was taken to a convenient part of the beach at high tide. Next day, when the tide receded, it was shared out in creelfuls, then taken to the roadside and finally carted home. It was hard work for little return.

The crofters also gathered another kind of seaweed called *feamainn chirean*, which grew on the rocks just below high-water mark. It was hard curly stuff about six inches long. It was boiled and given to the cattle in their feed.

Perhaps, however, the most valuable flotsam in the isles was timber. Timber was very scarce, and apart from a small plantation within the castle grounds, there is practically none. The early bird catches the worm, and so the beachcomber was on the job at the screich of dawn. Sometimes he was lucky, sometimes not. If he found any timber he dragged it up above the high-water mark and left it there until he had time to collect it. Anything found above high-water mark was not touched by others, as it was an indication that someone had already found it and dragged it up.

I remember two outstandingly good hauls of timber. One was when a Baltic timber-ship went ashore on the Braighe, and the other when the *Esther Maria* went on the Sgeir Mhor in Stornoway harbour. Both misfortunes were godsends to the crofters, and there was hardly a ditch, drain, or barn in my village but was piled with the gains. The whole deck cargo of the *Esther Maria* had to be jettisoned before the tugs got her off. The timber came ashore on the Mol Beag, or Little Beach, and when seen higgledy-piggledy as the tide left it, one would never believe that the deck of a ship could hold so much. There were boards and planks of all sizes piled up to a height of fifteen feet along a mile of shore. Indeed a sight for the gods! The Customs put two local men in charge, but I did not envy their job. When darkness came two men could not effectively watch a mile of open lonely shore. Everybody who could crawl, from nine years to ninety, was there.

Not all the timber was taken during the darkness, however. Some people went down during daylight and asked the watchers for just a board or two to make a cradle, or just a small piece to make a spurtle, while another, with a wink at his neighbour, wanted just enough to make a violin! But the watchers well knew that these were merely excuses to have a look round to spot the type of stuff they would come for at night.

After a week's time, a rumour went round that the Customs were going to search all houses. Thatched cottages which had been lined with the timber were soon covered over with wallpaper; stacks of straw were taken asunder and filled up with wood; newly-built sheds were hastily tarred over; new floors were rapidly covered with anything at all; while all the drains and ditches dividing croft lands were filled up with planks and boards. But the

Customs never came. A year later hen-sheds and outhouses sprang up like mushrooms, and the village had an air of great prosperity.

I remember an occasion when a ship, on a voyage from the Faeroes, was forced to throw overboard hundreds of sheep. She had struck bad weather and had run out of water and feeding-stuff and the sheep were dying. The authorities at Stornoway refused to allow any of the sheep to be landed, so the ship went about a mile outside the harbour and dumped them all overboard. A few sheep came ashore alive. The crofters immediately saw an opportunity here. Many went to the shore with their sheep shears and came home laden with bags of wool. Others took a whole sheep home and replenished their scanty larders. The carcases soon began to decompose on the shore, and eventually a squad had to go round and bury them.

A live whale was stranded on the beach one Sunday morning. That was a great novelty, for although we had seen scores of whales playing in the water, we had never seen one ashore. It was a small specimen, just over twenty feet. It was soon put an end to by the crofters with scythes and spades. There were hopes that the fish offal factory would use the body, but they did not want it. The boys, who thought the beast was dead, had a competition as to who would walk barefoot along its back. But it was not quite dead, and threw Iain Ruadh several feet into the air with a flip of its tail.

The carcase lay on the beach for weeks and the sickening stench could be smelt a mile away.

16

ROCK FISHING IN THE ISLES

The Western Isles were a boys' paradise. Everything that was attractive to a young growing boy was there: fishing, nesting, bathing, etc. Fishing, of course, was priority number one, and young boys of seven years fished regularly off the rocks. I am referring to my boyhood years around the turn of the century, when the sea was teeming with fish, when cares and worries did not exist for us, and before the Minch was swept clean by English trawlers from Fleetwood, Hull and Grimsby.

Strangely enough, the boys of my village did not go in for trout fishing, although there were plenty of good trout lochs within easy reach. We did occasionally find a salmon or two that had taken the wrong turning or one that had been killed by an otter. The otter sometimes kills for the sake of killing, takes one clean bite out of the back of its victim and leaves it. Compared with sea angling, trout-fishing to us was not attractive, and as we did not fish for sport but for the table, what was a dozen or two of trout compared with the same number of haddock, saith or mackerel, and perhaps, most exciting of all, the chance of landing a big chap, a cod, ling, conger or lythe?

Our first introduction to fishing was at about seven years of age when we fished in a comparatively safe place for cuddies, with a bit of string and a hook. Most of us had fallen in at some time or other and had managed somehow to scramble out again. I knew one boy of ten years who had been in eight times. During my time of residence in the isles, over fifty years, I can only recollect one drowning accident in the village.

All the cuddies we caught were put in a pool on the rocks, where we watched them swimming around among the dulse, seaweed and sea anemones. We hardly ever got sufficient of them to take home. At any rate, we were discouraged by our parents from taking them home with the remark 'Na marabh mathair na tradhad' (Don't kill the mother of the ebb). We hardly knew what it meant then, but it is only too well understood in the isles, where the scarcity was intensified by the taking of immature fish. A Gaelic proverb says, 'Where there is no young there will be no old'.

Our great day as boys was the day we aspired to a real rod, a bamboo one about fifteen feet long. It had no reel; the line just wound around it. We were then able to take our place on a recognised fishing ledge along with the older men. Later, we learned that the tide and the weather had a great deal to do with it, and as there were plenty of good fishing ledges, it became a simple matter to choose a ledge suited to the wind and tide. The Sgeir Fhaide was the favoured one, or, if the wind was too southerly, Creag an South or An Dun. There was a sheer drop of five or six fathoms from these ledges down to the clean sandy bottom below. The rock itself was well covered with barnacles and seaweed which afforded good cover for the lurking lythe.

On suitable evenings we fished with flies. We made these ourselves by securing a bit of gull's or goose's feather firmly to the shaft of the hook and nearly covering the barb. Sometimes a bit of coloured thread was added to make it attractive. Six flies were attached to the one line at intervals of about twelve to eighteen inches. A light sinker was used and the rod moved backwards and forwards above the water. The flies were rarely more than one foot under the water and were used mainly for cuddies, saith or mackerel. It was great sport when six were hooked, but we rarely chanced six as there was a danger of the line snapping and losing the lot. At times, however, it could not be avoided and great care and patience had to be exercised then, particularly when lifting them out of the water.

Sometimes we took the small flies off and fitted on a larger hook covered with a strip of red cycle inner tubing for lythe fishing. A heavier sinker was used here and the line dragged along the surface as for the flies. Catches of a score of lythe could be had by this method over the sunken reefs in an evening's fishing.

I noticed during a later visit to Lewis that the boys did not use the cycle rubber or flies the way we did. They had a heavy sinker on and worked the flies up and down in the water. They said it fished better that way, as they could get the fish at any depth whereas by our method we only attracted those near the surface.

If the evening was not suitable for the flies, we used bait, a foot or two off the bottom. Herring or mackerel bait was best for lythe or saith, but cockles or limpets were used when these were not available. Some, however, swore by crab bait. The back of the crab was broken and as much as possible of the soft pulpy meat extracted. It was most difficult to get it to stay on the hook, but we solved this difficulty by wrapping it around with wool. It was excellent for lythe and rock cod.

Just as the sun would be setting, the cuddies which swarmed around the shores began to play. When in that mood, they would not look at bait but would take the flies. The sea boiled with them, bubbles bursting all over the place. Shortly after, as it got dark, they began to shoal, making their way like armies on the march into the shallow and more sheltered waters. Instinct seemed to tell them they were safe from the bigger fish in the shallower waters.

It was most exciting to watch them at this stage, millions

of them it seemed, head to tail, hugging the rocks on their way to safety. This was the time we got our biggest hauls of cuddies. We used a *poca tabh* or sea bag. This was a net like an inverted cone hanging from a large hoop of strong fencing wire. The wire was about four or five feet in diameter, and the net hung from it like a child's butterfly or minnow net. Four strong strings supported the wire from a firm pole about seven or eight feet long. The pole was held between the legs and supported with the hands.

The operator occupied a quiet part of the ledge well away from the rod fishermen. Beside him was a small pail of cold cooked potatoes left over for that purpose from the day's dinner. His net was put out, the pole between his legs, and he leaned forward in a half-crouched position. It was not yet dark and shoaling had not yet commenced. He would chew up his cold potatoes and spit them out in tiny fragments over the top of the net. Straggling cuddies gathered around to snatch the titbits, and when the fisher thought a big enough number was swimming over his net he hauled quickly up and got a dozen or two with each haul. He could fill his pail quite easily without waiting for the shoaling.

But the fun really began with the shoaling. A sentry was placed at the extreme end of the rock to watch for the first shoal. He gave the warning, 'Here she comes, John'. The man with the net adjusted his footing and waited until the bulk of the shoal was over the net. He hauled up quickly and landed a pailful at a time. To save time, they were poured out on the rock as it was possible to get two hauls out of the same shoal. The small boys had a great time catching them and putting them in a bag.

Sometimes the shoal was lost as there were others interested in it as well. The lythe lurked in the tangle and would dash up like streak lightning amongst them and then the shoal scattered quickly. The lythe erred at times and made for the bottom over the net and found itself in the bag along with its intended victims.

A boll bag full was usually a night's fishing with the *poca tabh*. The cuddies were boiled and cooked along with the livers and were excellent fare, the juice also making a lovely thin soup. When they were very plentiful, many crofters salted them and ate them with potatoes in the winter.

In the month of July, the seas around the isles were teeming with the young newly-hatched spawn of the fish. They were known in Lewis as *siol* or seed. There were countless numbers about two inches long. They swam about in dense shoals waiting probably to grow up, and during that time it was a marvel that any of them survived at all, as they were the constant prey of mackerel and saith. No sooner were they on the surface to escape those than the sea birds—puffins, guillemots and the various types of gulls—were on top of them. During the nesting time, these birds could be seen with mouthfuls of them hanging from their beaks. How they managed to catch the extra ones without losing those they already had in their beaks continued to amaze us.

Eventually, the shoals of 'fry' found their way into all the small coves and bays even up to the point where the waves lapped the shore. So voracious were the mackerel that they ran themselves ashore on the shingle in their efforts to get at the fry. It was interesting to watch the skua, or Dirty Allan as it was locally called, during this period of plenty. It cannot fish for itself, so it hovered around until it saw a satisfied gull or tern flying quietly to some isolated rock to digest its meal. The skua chased it around, harassing and pecking at it until the gull disgorged its half-digested meal. The skua immediately dived down and scooped it all up before it reached the water. I have never seen the skua tackling the puffin or the guillemot. It probably knew that these could take evasive action by diving quickly.

17

LOBSTERS AND CRABS

Lobsters and crabs were very plentiful in the isles; the former were an asset, but the crabs to most fishermen were a nuisance. Lobsters were caught in traps or pots. A pot, somewhat like a cage, had two 'doors' and at times just one. The fishermen made their own from odd bits of timber found on the shore.

One fisherman I knew worked thirty pots, all made by himself. He had a small Norwegian skiff with an outboard motor. The motor he carried home every night. He worked alone and always made sure his engine was working before he left home. He had a barrel full of water in which he tested the motor at the back of the byre. A stick was put across the mouth of the barrel, and the engine was clamped on to it. Thus, at least he knew that it was working before he left home. He worked alone with the boat and knew too much about the sea and its moods to take chances with it.

He also used to shoot half-a-dozen flounder nets off the shore, and they provided him with bait for his pots and an ample supply of plaice, sole, turbot and skate with perhaps an odd cormorant or two thrown in. His great bogey was crabs, the big edible brown crab about seven by five inches in area on the back. They just made a mess of the nets as they rolled themselves in an effort to escape. The nets became a bundle of knots.

When that happened, he would take the tiller and smash them to pulp and extricate them in small pieces. I heard him mutter in his exasperation one day, 'If I could get down where you are for a short time with a potato masher, I would soon make short work of your broad backs'. Even those he got out whole from his pots were thrown aside for anyone who wanted them. They were not worth marketing from the isles in those days, for they did not last long before going bad.

He was getting an average of a dozen lobsters each day. Many pots would be empty but others would have two or even three. The pot or trap would be hauled up, the lobster taken out, the bait adjusted and then it was thrown overboard again. The whole operation took only about five or six minutes. In fine weather it was quite a pleasant job, but even then it was precarious work. The pots had to be set amongst hidden reefs and skerries, and the ground swell even in good weather might throw the boat against the rocks.

In a sheltered cove near the shore he had a large wooden box anchored. Here he kept his lobsters alive until he had a few dozen. Before they were put in the box the big nippers were securely tied with string, as the lobsters often attacked and damaged one another. Some fishermen, however, cut one of the joints in the big nipper and this rendered the claw useless. The cutting of the muscle had an advantage over severing with string. In the event of the box snapping its moorings in heavy weather, the lobsters could escape. The fishermen maintained that the severed muscle healed up in a few days and thus the lobster was able to survive, whereas the others were sure to perish.

Few people realise that the lobster is one of the swiftest creatures of the sea. An old Gaelic proverb says: 'An giomach, an runach, 's an ron, Tri seoid na mara' (The lobster, the mackerel and the seal—three heroes of the deep). Those who have had the good fortune to see these in their native element can testify to the truth of the old saying. The lobster does not swim forwards, but backwards. It keeps flapping its powerful tail and hops at terrific speed. Its movements on the rocks, however, are slow and clumsy. During the day, it prefers to hide in some crevice or under a big stone with its nippers out in front.

Islesmen were familiar with its habits, and as boys we used to go down to the shore when the tide was out and prepare beds for them. The big boulders would be levered up and a small stone put underneath so as to leave an attractive nook below. Next day at low tide, these nooks were examined and we invariably came home with a lobster.

I had one very interesting day with the lobster fisherman. He got his usual dozen that day, but one pot he pulled up contained a four-foot-long eel. A great fight seemed to have gone on in the pot, for the eel showed scars of battle. Many white spots could be seen on its body where the lobster had got a hold and the skin had been torn. My friend soon made short work of it. He killed it, split it open and used it as bait. Plaice, he said, made the best bait of all, but anything white attracted the lobster, and when bait was scarce he had even used broken plates and old white collars and had caught lobsters.

He drew my attention to a flock of squawking seabirds: gulls, guillemots, puffins and several gannets wheeling around about a quarter of a mile away. 'That is a shoal of herring or mackerel they are after,' he said. 'Just you watch the gannets.' And they were beautiful to watch. From a height about a hundred feet, they dived with folded wings and perfect accuracy into the middle of the shoal. I noticed a smile spreading over my friend's face. 'There is your dive-bombing,' he said. 'The scientists think they have discovered something, but the gannets have been doing it for centuries.'

As I watched, the dive-bombing continued steadily, spurts appearing in the water like shellfire. No sooner did the gannet disappear than it was up again, briefly pausing on the surface to stretch its gullet and swallow its catch, then it was airborne again, wings spread, ready for the next dive. What a voracious appetite! Gannets, however, sometimes err in judging the depth of water. When the shoal of fish passed over a submerged reef with only two or three feet of water on top, the bird dived to its death on the rocks below.

The lobster fisherman also showed me a small octopus which was entangled in one of his pots. I shuddered at the way he handled the slimy, crawling creature as he let it sprawl over his bare arm. The octopus has a head like a torpedo and its tentacles trail behind when it is swimming. He pointed out the tiny holes in the head through which water is ejected, thus giving it a forward movement. Again he had his sly dig at modern science—'Jet propelled,' he pointed out. 'Nature had it before they ever thought of it.' He then placed it in the water and asked me to watch. For a moment or two it lay limp in the water and then, emitting a cloud of black inky substance, disappeared behind it. Again the smile of contempt spread across his face, 'There is nothing new in the world.' I nodded in assent at the deep philosophy and knowledge of this fisherman who had learned how to use his eyes.

I collected a small pailful of crab nippers and made my way slowly home across the moor. The Americans were based on the nearby 'drome and had built experimental huts on the moor. I was stopped by a sergeant who demanded to know what I had in the pail. He had a look. 'Gee,' he muttered in surprise, 'where did you get these?' I told him a fisherman had given them to me down in the village. 'Can I get some?' he enquired. 'Take the lot,' I replied. He was astonished when I told him I wanted nothing for them and insisted on offering me money out of all proportion to the value, but I persistently refused.

Lobsters and Crabs

Then I had a brainwave. 'Listen,' I said, 'petrol is rationed and scarce; if you could give the fisherman an odd gallon of petrol, you can get as many crabs as you like and probably an occasional lobster as well.'

I suggested meeting him next day and carrying the tin of petrol to the village. He did not seem impressed with this idea, paused for a moment and decided that that method was too slow. 'I'll tell you what,' he rapped out, 'I'll deliver the goddam stuff.'

Next day when I went down to the village, a small jeep was parked on the shore, and there he was making a deal with my friend. The can of petrol was there and two dozen cigars for me for my share in the transaction. Although my time on the island was shortly to end, I was sure that the fisherman would have an ample supply of petrol and 'the Yank' a constant supply of crabs, while I dreamed of the Hebrides through the haze and aroma of choice cigars.

18

MUSKINS AND CLAMS

In my native village, muskins or razorfish were the only shellfish used for home consumption. They could only be found with the lowest spring ebbs in March and April, and only villages which had the good fortune to have an *oitir* nearby sought them at all. In fact, there were villages in Lewis which did not know what muskins were. In parts of Scotland they were called muskins, obviously an anglicised attempt at the Gaelic form *muirsgean*, from *muir* meaning the sea, and *sgian*, a knife; in other words, a sea knife, or, as commonly called in English, razorfish. An *oitir* is a sandbank which is only visible with the lowest spring tides.

The moment the top of the bank came in sight, men and women waded out while the water was still two or three feet deep in the channel. This was to enable them to spend as long a period as possible on the bank before the tide turned. For the same reason they stayed on the bank until it was nearly awash, and then waded across the channel with the water up to their waists. The spade was then put through the handle of the pail and carried over the shoulder.

The muskin, particularly if the weather was sunny, came up to the top of its burrow and stayed there until it was disturbed. With the least motion of the sand, up went a squirt of water and it sucked itself to the bottom of the burrow about a foot and a half down, according to the depth of sand. The moment a squirt went up, that was the sign that a muskin was there, and rapid digging was necessary to keep up with it. Some people put the spade down ahead of the muskin in order to jam it or block its way, but this method usually broke the shell, and a person with a pailful of broken shells was the victim of all kinds of smart observations by the neighbours.

Dogs were not allowed on the bank as they raced around and disturbed the razorfish, which immediately sucked itself down to the bottom. The sucker was at the lower end and could be stretched from four to six inches ahead of itself, and then, snail-like, it dragged the rest of its body behind it. It was not, however, a slow motion; it could move to the bottom very rapidly.

A peculiar custom was that everybody whistled when pulling up the razorfish. This was supposed to make it let go its hold and be pulled up more easily. One had to be very careful when pulling out the fish, for it would be hanging on for dear life with its sucker and if pulled up too rapidly, the 'meat' would be left behind and the digger found himself with an empty shell.

So, the pull had to be gentle and the whistling had to continue. The expert could tell the correct strength of pull, for he could feel it letting go its hold. It was more or less like playing a fish. Unless it was tackled very patiently, both fish and line would be lost.

Some people, however, did not take a spade at all. They waded around on the outer edge of the bank where the water was up to a foot deep. Experience had taught them how to get the razorfish in the water. When the razorfish came to the top in the water it disturbed the sand and left a small saucerlike hollow about two inches wide. The expert recognised the hollow and saw the dark speck in the centre of it where the small feelers protruded. Very gently he put down his finger alongside of it and jammed it against the burrow. Even the gentlest touch did this. With the other hand he scooped a little of the sand away until he got a firm hold of it. Then a gentle pull and a steady whistle brought it slowly to the surface. He could fill his bucket in half the time it took the man with the spade, and none of them was broken. Three or four could be picked up in this way without moving a step.

A friend who had spent a holiday in the Channel Islands told me she had seen her landlord there get them by pouring salt into the hole. I was not sure whether this was a leg-pull or not but decided to give it a trial. So, with the first suitable tide, off I went armed with a small bag of table salt. The ebb was rather wet and the salt dissolved before it could penetrate into the hole. However, I found a dry patch and poured a spoonful of salt into the first hole I found.

A few moments passed and I concluded at first it was not a muskin's hole at all, but I was soon enlightened, for up came the muskin and squirted right into my face which was quite near the hole as I wanted to see all that was happening. Down it went again clean out of sight, up again, and it fired another shot. This happened twice, but I caught a hold of it the third time and pulled it out as I was there for a meal and not for sport. I thought that two chances were fair enough as it might not come up a third time. So, it would appear that the Channel Islander was one ahead of the Hebridean. I rather think the explanation is that the fish found the concentrated salt so briny and nauseating that it came to the top to squirt as much as possible of the unpleasant stuff out of its burrow.

A remarkable phenomenon occurred occasionally in Broad Bay on the east side of Lewis. It happened only twice during my lifetime. The crofters called it *bristeadh na traghad* or the breaking of the ebb. When it happened, vast numbers of shellfish, particularly spoutfish, were cast up high and dry by the tide.

Villagers gathered from far and near when the news

went round, and everybody, old and young, who could carry any kind of receptacle, went there—women with creels, men with sacks or wheelbarrows and boys with baskets or pails gathered to get their share of the harvest. Even cartloads of them were carried away. The women with the creels and the men with the sacks had the worst time, for the shells were dripping wet and clothes were soon soaked through to the skin. The sea birds had a glorious time and their squawking could be heard at night miles away.

The older crofters used to say the ebb had become overcrowded with shellfish and this was nature's way of thinning them out. Only on two occasions had I seen this remarkable phenomenon, but both occasions had something in common. The wind blew strongly from the north-east and it was during the spring tides. What I suspect happened was that a strong nor-easter coincided with a low spring ebb, and the continuous pounding on the sand by mighty waves shifted the shellfish's covering of sand and left them bare and at the mercy of the incoming tide.

The crofters first scalded the shells with hot water. This opened all the shells and the meat was then easily extracted. They were then put in a pie dish or casserole with milk and seasoning and left to simmer in a slow oven. They were delicious to taste and even better than clams or oysters. The crofters tried salting or pickling them but after two or three days the flavour was gone. I heard of one instance where a fair-sized pearl was found in one.

Clams too were a great delicacy but they were not so numerous and therefore much harder to get. They never allowed themselves to ebb, and even with the lowest spring tides were, as a rule, in at least a fathom of water. They could be seen lying flat on the sandy bottom. A boat was needed for this job and a long pole with a hoop and net like a child's butterfly net. They were scooped up from the bottom with the net.

The shell was partially open when lying on the bottom but the moment it felt anything approaching, the shells snapped quickly together. The sea water was rapidly ejected between the shells, thus giving a kind of jet-propelled hop. The fishermen, however, approached them from behind and the hop just landed them in the net. The upper shell of the clam was always kept, and at least one could be found in every crofter's house. It was used to skim the cream off the basins of milk.

Winkles and limpets were plentiful, but apart from an occasional meal, they were seldom collected except for small line bait.

The women from the villages skirting Broad Bay walked seven to ten miles each morning with a creel on their backs, full of haddocks to sell in Stornoway, and returned home with sufficient bait of limpets, cockles and mussels for the next day's baiting of the lines. Nothing was ever wasted in their lives, not even time, for as they walked the long miles their hands were also busy, knitting for the family.

19

IN DEEPER WATERS

All the villages in Lewis except two are on the coast, hence all the crofters fished as well as worked the land. They all had fishing gear of some kind: nets, lines or rods. The *lion beag* or small line was the one used most, because in the main it was used for inshore fishing, and bait for it could be easily provided on the shore. It was called the small line, although it was by no means small, to distinguish it from the *lion mor* or great line, which had much heavier hooks and was used for deeper waters.

The *lion beag* was a long line with snoods and hooks attached at intervals of about a fathom. It had, as a rule, four hundred hooks and was baited with shellfish: mussels, cockles or limpets. The snoods were of cord or hair, but the hair was considered the better.

During the winter the young men and boys passed the time making snoods from horse's hair. Several hairs were first twisted together and then two of these were rolled together to make the final snood. They were laid on the bare knee and rolled along with the palm of the hand. Horse's hair had better fishing properties than the cord because it would stretch a little when tugged and was not so ready to snap as the cord. Also, when the line was lying on the bottom, it tended to float and fished better than the cord which lay dead on the bottom.

The small line was kept in a *sguil* or long shallow basket, and when baited, all the hooks were arranged in rows along the shallow end. Baiting was a long tedious job and meant a trip to the ebb the day before. All the mussels had to be shelled, but the cockles and limpets could be scalded and the meat easily extracted. Baiting was usually done at night by the fire when a few of the ceilidh folk were willing to give a hand. Mussel was the best bait for haddocks, but if herring or mackerel bait was available it was used and was considered very good.

Lines were set at dusk or at dawn. Most boats carried five or six lines, thus giving a stretch of over two thousand hooks. The best fishing grounds were known, and where the area was limited, the lines were shot backwards and forwards over the same area, taking care not to shoot one end of the line over another.

On arrival at the fishing ground, the buoy, usually a cow's bladder, was thrown overboard with a sinker of stone. Bearings were taken on the land and the lines shot. The newest lines were put at each end and the older or weaker ones put in the middle. A break in the middle was not so serious as a break in an old line at each end. In the event of a break, they went back to the last buoy. With five or more lines aboard no time was given for the lines to fish. It was considered that the first line shot had fished its maximum before all the others were set, and so sail was set immediately for the first buoy.

Four oars were used for hauling and the boat's head kept in the direction of the lines. The man hauling gave all the instructions as regards rowing: 'Not so strong on this side. A little stronger on the other,' etc. It was a lovely sight when you looked down and saw about half-a-dozen fish circling round and round as the line was hauled up. But it was not such an easy job for the man who had to take them off the hooks. Haddocks and whiting were not so difficult to take off, although in most cases the hook was right down in the pit of the stomach. The throat of the fish was then cut and the hook was more easily extracted, but it was a different matter when the fish happened to be an eel, a skate or a dogfish. They all have formidable teeth and great care must be exercised. The method of controlling the eel was to give it a blow on the vent with the tiller. All kinds of fish can be caught with the small line, big and small, and even starfish, crabs and clams.

When the shore was reached, the boat was dragged a bit up on to the beach and all the fish thrown on to the shingle. The fish was then shared out according to the number in the crew, plus a share for the boat. It was customary also to have a share for the needy, a custom which I am sorry to say has now died out.

When each share of fish was completed, each man picked up a token from the beach, an empty mussel or limpet shell, a stone, bit of stick or anything that was lying about on shore. These were all handed to one man who was not aware of what any particular person had picked. He threw one on each lot of fish, and wherever your token had fallen, that was your share of the fish.

Sometimes a different method of sharing was used. One man was asked to turn his back while another shouted, 'Who will have this?' 'Domhnull Ban,' came the answer. 'And this?' 'Uilleam Beag', and so on until a share was allocated to every member of the crew.

There was one occasion, however, when this method did not work. There were four men in the crew and two small codlings made up the full catch. On the way to the shore they decided that it was not worth while making four shares and that they would cast lots for the two. Duncan and Murdo readily agreed as they were both from the same house and thus had a fifty per cent chance. But they did not reckon with smart Alex, one of the crew. When the lots were ready to be cast, Alex said, 'I'll turn my back'. He did so and then somebody shouted, 'Who will have this?' 'Angie,' came the reply. 'And this?' 'Myself,' came the answer. And so Duncan and Murdo from the same house got nothing.

The women were usually on the shore with their creels and helped in drawing up the boats. They carried the fish home on their backs while the men carried the *sguil* and cables. The crabs were left to the small boys to play with. They used the large nippers as pipes and smoked peat fibre.

The great lines had much larger hooks and were baited with herring or mackerel. A whole herring made two or at most three baits. The lines were carried in a large high basket with the hooks stuck to corks fitted around the rim. They were set just like the small lines used in much deeper water, unless one had an occasional shot for eels or lythe along the rocks.

During my boyhood, curers had stations for salting the fish all round the island wherever fishing was being done. These salting houses had sleeping accommodation for the fishermen who were away from home for weeks at a time. Great hauls of ling, cod, halibut and roker were taken. On arrival the cook was the first man ashore, and several large ling and cod were thrown on the beach for cooking in the bothy.

He split them open, extracted the liver and roe and had a meal ready before the splitting and salting began. The curer bought all the cod and line, the rest being given to anybody who wanted it. It seemed strange that fish like halibut was not in great demand. The trouble was that halibut and skate could not be salted and thus could not be carried to the markets, in good condition. So there was ample to spare of these for everybody. In fact, halibut was often used as a skid to drag up the boat.

When the curer had a full cargo, his smack would arrive and all the salted fish were taken aboard. These were taken to a clean shingle beach and spread out each sunny day to dry. The beach in my own native village used to be covered with dried fish in the summer time for a distance of a quarter of a mile. As the fish dried, it became whiter and more attractive in appearance. As boys we used to walk barefoot on the fish on our way to town. So much for hygiene!

In the salting houses they practically lived on fish, oatmeal and fish liver, and the biggest delicacy of all was the fish stomach or head filled up with liver and oatmeal. A rope was stretched across the ceiling of the bothy and the filled spare stomachs were hung up like Christmas stockings. They were used as snacks between meals if one felt like it.

On the way to the fishing grounds each man carried a bannock of oat or barley bread with a thick smearing of butter and fish liver. Sometimes they had to row long distances, and then the bannock was placed between two folds of the oilskin on the seat. The heat of the body semi-baked the bannock and melted the liver so that the oil penetrated into the bread. It was nourishing and sustaining food.

Some types of fish that were very plentiful fifty years ago have now disappeared from the shores of Lewis altogether, such as hake and bream. Hake and bream could be fished with the rod off the rocks, but only on rare occasions, if ever, are any of these landed now at all. Bream travel in shoals and these were fished over hidden reefs where a strong tidal current was running. They were fished with the hand line, sinker and beam with two snoods. It was a great thrill when a shoal of bream struck the boat. It only lasted for a short time, and each person was eager to get as many out of it as possible while it lasted. Then they disappeared as mysteriously as they arrived. It was difficult to get them over the gunwale. The bream was weak in the jaw, and the moment it was lifted out of the water the jaw broke and the fish got away. Time was too valuable to use a gaff and it was more profitable to fish away even with the one snood than lose the whole shoal by fitting on another snood. It was a very attractive fish to look at, but its flesh was coarse and many people did not like it. But it was handy to have a barrel of them salted away for the lean days.

Salmon, of course, were forbidden, and any caught in the estuary of the river were supposed to be thrown back again into the sea. The estuary was a stretch of five or six miles from the river's mouth. And what was one to do with fish that seemed to have the freedom of the estuary and which meshed themselves in other folk's nets? I have seen dogfish thrown overboard, but never salmon. Salmon will occasionally take mussel or herring bait and there have been many isolated cases of boys landing them with rod and line on the rocks.

The only salmon river of any importance running into Stornoway harbour is the Creed. One year when there was not sufficient water in the river to enable the salmon to get up, the boys had a thrilling time. The salmon were floating about the bay with the dorsal fin showing above the water. They seemed half dazed, and it is said they later develop a pale spot on the back of the head and eventually die if they do not get up to the fresh water. The boys jigged dozens of them with the 'murderer'. That was the local name for three large hooks fixed back to back like a grapnel.

The king of the fishes among fishermen was the herring. It was more important than all the others put together. If it failed, the outlook in the isles would be a gloomy one. Probably the most beautiful sight connected with any type of fishing is a net full of silvery herring. Few people apart from fishermen have seen a live herring; it is very short-lived and is practically dead as soon as it drops out of the net. Other fishes like eels, flounders and whiting live for a long time after coming out of the water.

Nobody seemed to want mackerel, and Dutch smacks reaped a rich harvest of them during the summer fishing. The drifters landed a few baskets of them each day and sold them for what they could get to the Dutchmen. They gutted and salted them, and I am told they used them afterwards as bait for their lobster pots.

Sometimes flounder nets were set on the shore when the tide was out. If the crofter was able to get there before the next turn of the tide, and before the gulls were up, he was able always to get a few to keep the pot boiling. On level stretches of sand, the tide sometimes left large pools behind where many flounders were trapped until the turn of the tide. The boys tramped these pools and very often came home with a boiling of nice fresh flounders.

I don't know whether thunder affects fish, but it was a common experience to see the cuddies during thundery weather erect and motionless in the water with their heads pointing down.

20

IN THE PEATS

A common excuse for absence from school in my time was 'anns a mhonadh' (in the peats). Peats were as necessary as food, and whatsoever reasons there were for lack of the latter, there were no reasons for lack of the former. Lewis has been described as 'a peat floating in the Atlantic'. The description is fitting, as there are places where the moss is up to twenty feet deep.

Each village had an area allocated for peat-cutting as near the township as possible. The banks were usually about seventy yards long, ten yards apart, and running parallel with each other, sloping down the hill. The top layer of turf had first to be skinned off about one yard wide in order to lay bare the moss ready for the peat knife.

Peat-cutting day was one of the big days of the year. On that date a *sgiobadh* or crew of four, six or eight people gathered to do your cutting. That labour was repaid by you later by giving them a day. A peat-knife was operated by two people, one cutting and the other throwing out. Sometimes there were three or four cutters engaged on the same bank. The first pair took the top layer, cutting one peat deep, the second pair followed behind them and the third pair behind them, and so on, according to the number of irons on the job.

A peat measures about ten inches each way and about three to four inches deep. The first and second pairs of cutters must throw the peats out as far as possible in order to leave space for the third pair. The newly-cut peats are all handled on edge and never on the flat as they break very readily.

The difficulty with a four-peat-deep bank is the lack of space and the difficulty of throwing soft peat a long distance. In these cases a wall of peat was made on the higher bank, arranged in such a way that the wind could blow between them, but these peats when dry tended to stick to each other and were often broken before they could be pried apart.

There was great fun and hilarity on peat-cutting day, and although it was really hard work, it was looked upon as a picnic day. The whole family went, and all the utensils and food necessary for the outing were carried in creels to the banks. The children had the job of carrying the water from the nearest burn and collecting bits of sticks and old heather to get the fire going. Potatoes, herring, scones, oatcake and tea or milk were served, and they could not be served under better conditions. Joyful conversation and witty remarks flew all the time, and bursts of loud laughter could be heard all over the moor as some young man chased a coy maid, or as an S. O. S. went round to pull Brisgean's heifer out of the bog.

Was there any pleasure greater than walking barefoot over newly-cut peat? The finest carpet in a royal palace could not possibly give the comforting feel that a new peat gave to a boy, particularly if his feet had been hacked by the dry easterly winds of March. As boys, we loved to see our small footprints in the soft peat, and how easy it was to carve your name with your finger on dozens of them. When tired of carving, away we went to the next bank where a bull's eye was marked out as a target to throw stones at it. Each stone stuck where it hit, so that we saw the result of the shot and were thus able to correct the last effort. Some of the boys were most accurate, and the telegraph insulators suffered most from this training.

On herding days there was little else to do, and so the telegraph insulators became the target, not to be malicious or from lack of home tuition, but just a competition with your chum to see who was the more accurate.

I remember several boys in my village being taken to court and fined for breaking telegraph insulators. The chief witness against them was a tinker girl who was herself more accurate than any of the boys at breaking insulators. She avoided the village for some time until she thought the incident had been forgotten. But one day she arrived on the usual begging mission, and no sooner did her face appear in the doorway than Pohan, who happened to be sitting down to dinner, made a direct hit with a hot potato over her eye.

The tinkers themselves never cut peats. They seemed to think they were privileged to take as many as they required. They toiled not, neither did they spin, yet they never seemed to go short of fuel. The cutting of peats was at different times according to the district. Some districts cut them in April before they began the croftwork, while other districts preferred to finish off the essential part of the croftwork first.

After the cutting, the peats were allowed to lie until most of the moisture was absorbed. If the weather was favourable and the peats had a good dry bed, they were ready for the first handling about ten days later. As the old folk used to say, 'The skin has formed'. They also remarked about folk who went out to cut rather early before the moss was ripe and the peats would not have the same heating value.

When the peats are ready for handling they are put standing up in twos against each other and a third lying flat on top. This is known as *an togail*, the lifting. Next is the *rudhadh*, putting them in heaps of about a dozen peats. They were usually left in these heaps until they were carried to the roadside. In some districts, they made small *cruachan* or stacks of them on the bank.

All the peats had to be carried to the peat road on the moor. The road was just a track and could only be used in dry weather. The women did most of the creel work while the men used sacks or barrows. The latter as a rule were not very convenient if you were crossing at right angles to the run of the banks. A plank was needed to get over each and there might be a dozen banks between you and the road. The distance to the road sometimes was very long, and days of hard work were required before the final creel was by the roadside.

Then the day arrived for taking the peats home. A crew of at least five was required at the moor end and two or three to toss up at the home end. In wet weather more time was lost digging out the cart than was actually spent on the peats. The peats were stacked up in the cart, two people throwing in and three packing, one astride the shafts and one standing on each wheel. The load was piled up like a pyramid.

At the home end, the *bodach* (old man) was in charge. He built and supervised the stack. The sides and end were neatly packed and sloped gently in order to throw off the rain. The top was neatly closed with peats on the flat and the other end left open for taking peats away as they were needed during the winter. The *bodach* usually had an old tin can in a corner and kept count of the loads by dropping a pebble into it after each load. Thus he was able to keep a tally of the number of loads in the stack. Uilleam Ban's calculation, however, was upset when one of the village mischiefs dropped a handful of pebbles in the can unknown to him.

There were districts where carts were of little use for the peats. At Steinish, for example, they had to cross a mile of tidal sands before they could reach their peats. They could go only when the tide was out unless they took the long way round, involving two to three miles more travelling. It was the same coming back, and often they waited as long as possible and men and women would have to wade in places with the water up to their waists. When the peats were ready they were ferried across in boats. At other points on the west side of the island, the peats when dry were thrown into the burn, which carried them along to the village. They were then fished out at the other end.

In Lewis, forty to sixty cartloads was a good year's supply. There was no saving of peats, everybody had plenty, and roaring fires were on in all the houses. Each day, several creelfuls were stacked under the *leabaidh ard* (high bed) in the kitchen, and it was the duty of the person sitting nearest to it to see that the fire was well stoked. Some peats are better than others, and the deeper one goes in the bank, the better the peat. The best layer of all is the one nearest *an caoran dubh* (the black bit). It is nearly as good as coal.

If one visits the isles today, one will find that most of these methods have changed. In many districts the banks have become exhausted and much longer distances have to be travelled. In my own native village of Sandwick the peat banks are now five miles away. And what a transformation from the old days! The hilarity and general cooperation are gone. There is no 'day for day' as it used to be, but hard cash for everything. Winter fuel, for those who take advantage of cutting peats, is now counted in lorry loads, and no tin cans are needed to count the loads, as the total is about five as a rule, and most of the old *bodachs* are able to count as high as that without the can!

21

TALES OF THE CEILIDH HOUSE

The ceilidh was full and I counted nineteen people sitting around. The *being* (settle) was crowded, all the stools were occupied, some sat on peats, and a few more sat on the edge of the *leabaidh ard* (high bed) with their feet dangling. 'Come on,' said Uilleam Ruadh to the *Saighdear* (soldier), winking at the rest. 'Tell us about the time the cannibals ate you in the South Sea Islands.' 'No cannibal would eat you,' replied the Soldier, 'You are far too tough, but if you will tell us about the time you were drowned in the Red Sea, I'll tell you one first.' 'It's a bargain,' replied William. This was the story.

'Now, this is a true story, and I know you won't believe it. I was stationed once in Bermuda. It was a lovely spot like a fairy island with beautiful coral beaches and roads, and the weather was always like summer. There were winds and spirits in plenty and rum was very cheap. Some of the boys drank heavily at first and were deceived by the cheap wine. When you get drunk on wine, you only need a glass of water the following day to make you as bad as you were the day before. ('What a paradise,' muttered some-one.)

'Well, the rum got a hold of the cook and he was seldom sober. The cook is a very important man in a regiment and you cannot send him to jail or you get no breakfast next morning. He had the sense, however, to keep out of the way until he was sober.

'There were three sentry posts in the barracks, simply

called Number 1, Number 2 and Number 3. They were separated by about a hundred yards. Every house he passed, Number 1 sentry would call out to Number 2 'All is well'. Number 2 would answer the call and yell out, 'All is well at Number 2', and so on.

'The mortuary was at Number 3 post and it was that sentry's duty to reach it and knock at the door. Some of the younger lads were quite scared to do this, and often rather than reach the mortuary door and knock it, they preferred to throw a stone at it from a distance.

'One dark night, when Number 2 called out, 'All clear at Number 2', there was no answer. He yelled several times and then reported it to Number 1. The matter was then reported to the sergeant on duty and the guard was called out to investigate. When they arrived at Number 3's post, they found him lying unconscious at the mortuary door. He was removed immediately to hospital and was sufficiently recovered next day to tell them that he had seen a ghost coming out of the mortuary.

'As I told you before, the cook was never sober, so when he had too much to drink, he knew that his best plan was to get out of the way somewhere. If he went to the quarters he would be spotted during the officer's rounds. There was only one safe place in the barracks where he would not be disturbed and that was the mortuary. Two or three hours' sleep and he would be ready for duty in the morning. The cook is the first up in the camp.

'When Number 3 rattled the door very early in the morning, the cook was awakened by the noise. He still had on his white cap and coat when he opened the door. 'What's the time, chum?' he asked the astonished sentry, whereupon the sentry passed out immediately. And that was the reason why there was no answer from Number 3 that morning.' 'That is as sure as I am sitting here,' said Torquil, 'and I wasn't the sentry, either. Now it's your turn.'

'Well,' said Uilleam, 'I was never in Bermuda, but I have been in Harris and Mull. I was one day crossing in the boat between Mull and Oban. There was just a small sea running and there were quite a few passengers aboard. There was a well-dressed gentleman smoking his pipe and pacing backwards and forwards on the deck. I discovered afterwards he was not a gentleman at all, for he had the Gaelic the same as myself. However, he put me in the notion for a smoke, and when I put my hand in my pocket, what do you think? I had left my pipe and tobacco in the pocket of my other jacket.'

'Don't be telling the lies,' interjected Torquil, 'You never had any jacket but the one.'

'Well, I had not the face to ask him for a chew, but I went over and spoke to him. "Good morning," I said, "I think she will be in on time today." "I think she will," he replied, and I knew as soon as he spoke his tongue was as thick as my own is in the English. Well, we got talking, and when he had refilled his own pipe, he offered me a fill out of his *spliuchan* [tobacco pouch]. I told him that I had left my own tobacco in my other jacket, but if I could take a chew I would be very grateful. I took as much as I could lift between my two fingers, but it was cut stuff and it spread all over my mouth. He was a fine man, and I thanked him kindly and hoped the same thing would happen to him as happened to myself.

'And what was that?' he asked. 'Listen,' I said, 'I once dreamed that I died and that I was carried through the sky for a long distance by an angel. At last we came to a great wall, the walls of heaven. Instead of a gate, there was a gap in the wall, and there stood a mighty pair of scales and an angel on each side of them.

'One angel was black and the other white, and the black one was putting all the bad deeds I had done on earth on the one side of the scales and the white one was doing the same with all the good deeds I had done on the other. The dreadful moment arrived when both books were exhausted, and do you know, the scales stood still, then settled down as if by the weight of a hair on the side of the black one. The white angel looked pityingly as if she was sorry that such a fine-looking man should be lost. And so, in desperation, she began turning over the pages again in case she had missed anything, and there, at the foot of a page, she discovered that I had once given a chew of tobacco to a poor old man. She put this on the scales and down they went on the white side. And I was saved, saved, sir, by a chew of tobacco.'

'Well told,' muttered Torquil, 'You had a narrow shave that time, and that is just about your worth anyway. But tell me—and you a fisherman, too . . . which side is the flounder's mouth twisted, to the right or to the left?' Uilleam twisted his moustache first to one side then to the other and finally decided he was not very sure.

'How should I know anyway? I have not seen all the flounders in the sea.'

'Tell me, then, if you call yourself a fisherman, why the flounder has a twist in its mouth.'

'The mermaid on Leac na Maighdean [the flat rock of the maiden] told my grandfather all about that,' replied Uilleam. 'Now this is as true as . . . (He was standing up, then sat down) as true as I am sitting here.'

'You see, the fishes of the sea had a great meeting once upon a time to choose one of themselves as King of the Fishes. This great meeting was held in Broad Bay, the finest spawning bay they could find in the whole of Scotland. They gathered from all directions, and there were even some gurnets there from Loch Eirisort in Lochs [Torquil was a Lochs man and Uilleam had to get a dig in when he could.]

'Many of the fishes thought they would be chosen; the

mackerel for its great speed, symmetry and colouring; the halibut for its great size and tastiness of flesh; the eel for its subtlety and variety of life; the bream for its heavy scales and beautiful golden colouring, and so on.

'However, when the meeting ended, none of those with outstanding qualification of speed, strength, beauty, etc. was chosen, but the humble herring, because it was not a cannibal, because of its vast numbers and because of its great use to man. The humble herring was proclaimed King of the Sea.

'Naturally, many of the other fishes were disappointed and turned back home. They met the flounders, who were late going to the meeting. You see, they had no clocks in Lochs and did not know the time. Either that, or the clocks they had were too old and could not stand up to the new time. The flounders, in great concern, asked if the meeting was over and who had been chosen, having great hopes of being elected themselves. When told that it was all over and that the herring had been chosen as the King of the Sea, they were so disappointed that they put a twist in their mouths, and that twist has remained in their mouths to this day.'

22

OLD CURES AND BELIEFS

Modern science and education have killed out many of the old cures and beliefs, but it is amazing the number of them that remain even now. Old traditions die hard.

Tinneas an righ, the disease of the king—that is to say, king's evil or scrofula—was cured by the touch of the seventh son. My wife's brother was a king's evil doctor and I had the opportunity of seeing many cases of this illness being treated. The qualification was to be the seventh son or daughter in the family, with no intervening child. In some cases, one intervening daughter was recognised. Some people maintained that the curing power was far stronger if there was an intervening daughter.

People came long distances to be cured of their ailment. I voice no opinion on the practice, but I know that it worked successfully. My father had a boil which refused to heal up. It was lanced by the doctor several times, and each time it filled up again. Nor did my father believe in the seventh son doctor, but out of mere curiosity he decided to give the notion a trial.

The patient had to call early in the morning before partaking of any food. The doctor took a bowl of warm water, dipped his fingers in it and then rubbed them very gently backwards and forwards three times over the boil. This had to be done on three successive mornings. Treatment by the seventh son cured my father's boil.

A seventh daughter, as already mentioned, could also be a doctor. I knew of one old lady who practised the art. One case was actually brought along after the old lady had died. It was during the interval between the death and the burial. A very young boy who had scrofula at the time was taken to the house where the body was still lying in the coffin. The hand of the dead lady was dipped in a bowl of water and rubbed three times on the child's face, enough, I should say, to cure anything, and also to scare a young boy out of his wits! In this case, the hand was gloved and one might have doubted its healing properties. The boy was, however, cured.

There were also rhymes and incantations. Styes were cured by incantation and a darning needle. This was done to my own eyes on more than one occasion. An old spinster did it in my case, and I do not know what qualifications she had for the job. She chanted the following incantation in Gaelic: 'Why should one stye come and not two, why should two styes come and not three, three and not four . . . ?' And so on until ten was reached. On reaching ten, the figures were reversed: 'Why should ten come and not nine, nine and not eight?' and so on down to one, the final count being: 'Why should a stye come at all?' All the time the darning needle was dabbed at the eye without actually touching it.

In like manner there was a rhyme for curing a swelling in the armpit. The swelling was called in Gaelic *mam*, probably from Latin *mamma*, a breast. I have never seen the cure effected, but I knew the old man in Laxdale who worked it, and I often begged his son to get the words of the rhyme before his father, who was old and frail, would die, but I was not successful. He used a hatchet and the sharp edge was pointed towards the swelling as he repeated his rhyme.

I knew one young girl of about ten years of age who took epileptic fits. I missed her from the village for a few days and asked her on her return where she had been. She said she had been down to the village of Back to see a doctor. This seemed strange to me as there were many doctors much nearer than Back. But it turned out that this was one of the old local 'doctors'. She told me that he had clipped her finger- and toe-nails and also cut some of her hair. This is probably a relic of the old Druidical customs of centuries ago.

Teinne De, God's fire—that is to say, shingles—was cured with the blood of a black cock or the blood of a Munro. Sprains were righted by tying a bit of the outermost thread of the weft tightly round the joint. To end lumbago, a person who was unnaturally born, that is, feet first instead of head first, had to stand on your back while you lay down on the floor.

Cuts and bruises were common ailments. For cuts a spider's web was used, or tobacco leaf, or *breid loisgte*, burnt cloth. The last-named was a piece of folded cloth with salt homemade butter in between. The tongs were put in the fire and the *breid* squeezed between the two 'pennies' of the tong-legs until the butter sizzled. It was then put on the wound as hot as one could bear it. For festering wounds it was quite good and drew any matter out.

Boys who were always barefoot suffered mostly from foot injuries. Split toe-nails, acquired through hitting them against stones, were always with us, but probably the worst of all were the hacks of March. In the dry spring weather the upper skin of the foot and between the toes became severely hacked. Nothing much could be done about the hacks and they were treated as a normal seasonal ailment. Bandaging was hopeless, because it never stayed on, and, even if it did, it was always soaking wet and was better off altogether. The boys grinned and bore it, but oh, what an agony it was to wash these hacked feet before bedtime.

Warts were cured by putting a bit of meat in a hole in a

wall, and as the meat rotted away, so did the wart. Washing the warts in lochs with certain properties was another cure.

Tonsilitis was treated with alum and pepper, but each village had its own expert for this disease. I was treated by one of these, who placed her finger down my throat and squeezed the swelling until it bled. I shall never forget it. Sterilising was unknown, and goodness knows where the finger had been before it went down my throat! Gargling with salt and water was also advocated.

For various types of stomach trouble the juice of *lus nan laogh*, coltsfoot, I presume, was drunk. Rheumatism, from which practically everybody suffered in later years, was eased by washing the feet with sea water. I knew one old lady who used to give a halfpenny to the boys to go to the shore for a pailful of sea water. But often they went to the nearest spring and old Annie did not seem to know a bit of difference.

An greim mor, the great pain, that is to say, pneumonia, took a heavy toll, and nothing could be done about it. One just heard the comment: 'He took the *greim*, and he only stood it for three days'. I have heard of blood-drawing being tried, but I have never known of any cases.

One woman I knew had leeches or *geallaichean*. While threshing corn, a grain of oats struck her in the eye. She went about for a time with a tea-leaf poultice. Eventually she lost the eye, but at one stage of her trouble the leeches were regularly applied to suck out the blood. She kept them in a jam jar in the window.

At that time there were only three or four doctors in Lewis to look after the health of twenty-eight thousand people. One doctor had a horse and trap donated to him by the people; another rode on horseback—Dr. Mackenzie, father of the well-known Agnes Mure Mackenzie. Doctors had a most difficult job. Roads were bad, distances were long, and, as a rule, medical help was not sent for until it was too late.

Pregnant women had an anxious time, as they worked hard on the croft until within hours of the birth of the child. Nor was there a recognised convalescing period, and they were at work again within a few days. I knew one woman who was up to her knees in salt water with her creel and sickle cutting seaweed three days after the birth of her child. She was in her eighties when she died.

There were no dentists, and I remember the first one who came round our district in the early days of the century. He had no dentist's chair or anaesthetic. His only implements were a pair of nippers or pliers and a jelly-jar for spitting into. He could have done quite well without the jelly-jar, for nobody was able to spit into it! With the excitement of the moment the saliva got sticky in the mouth and one could not aim at such a small target as the mouth of a jelly-jar. As boys, when we had toothache, we sucked cloves or smeared the gum over with a preparation called jelly-paste. If the tooth was loose, a string was tied round it and the other end of the string tied to the door-knob. Then somebody would suddenly shut the door before you were ready for the operation—and the tooth was out before you had time to funk it.

For drawing matter out of a festering wound, if poulticing was not satisfactory, a bottle was used. The bottle was filled with hot water up to the shoulders and its mouth placed firmly against the wound. Care had to be taken that no air got in at the mouth of the bottle. Then, as the water cooled, the condensed steam in the neck of the bottle left a vacuum, thus lessening the inside pressure. This caused a powerful sucking force from within the bottle. The method was a bit drastic, but I can assure you it drew all the matter out, and indeed it was difficult at times to get the bottle off.

Old Cures and Beliefs

Working at peats in dry windy weather caused much trouble through foreign matter getting into the eye. One way of clearing this was to stand facing the wind and blow the nose violently. Another was to bring the upper eyelid completely over the eye and move it round and round in all directions until the offending mote was got out. If these methods failed, there was always somebody in the village skilled in removing the irritant with the tongue. The tongue was put into the eye and moved backwards and forwards until the object was removed. This procedure was always effective, and the soft tongue did not in any way irritate the eye.

23

THE SUPERNATURAL

Nearly every village in the isles has its seer, and many Highland people are psychic and see things. As children we all believed in ghosts and feared them so much that we were afraid to go any farther than next door at night.

My mother often told me when I went out at night to be sure to keep to the side of the road in case I would meet a nocturnal funeral. These funerals always moved along the crown or middle of the road.

There were many instances of men meeting spirit funerals at night. To them there appeared no difference between such a funeral and any other funeral, except that it was night-time. Indeed, bodies arriving by the boat had to be transported home by night, and it was therefore difficult to recognise any difference between a real funeral and a spirit one.

It was not the custom in the isles to stand by the wayside with head uncovered when a funeral was approaching, but rather to take a turn at carrying, so helping the cortège on its way. Highland cemeteries were sometimes a long way off and every little help in carrying counted. Similarly, when a spirit funeral was met, the wayfarer took his turn as usual at carrying. It was all perfectly natural to him. He knew the people round about him and could even read the name of the deceased on the coffin-plate. He moved steadily on with measured step along with the rest. Eventually, the funeral would disappear when it came to a running stream, and the man found himself a long way from home on a lonely country road. Spirit funerals could not pass running water. Burns mentions in his poem *Tam o' Shanter*: 'A running stream they dare na cross'. I have been out at all hours of the night on very lonely roads in the isles and have never met or seen anything out of the ordinary. But then I might not be psychic.

A friend of mine, a schoolteacher who was inclined to laugh at these things, related to me the following experience he had. One Saturday morning he and the maid were cutting peats within twenty yards of the main road leading into the village. They had been working very hard and sat down on the bank for a short rest. 'Look,' said the maid, 'look at the funeral going out along the road.' Morrison looked and could see nothing. The maid gave the names of the people who were in attendance, and even told Morrison that he was there, naming the person he had as partner.

Morrison was convinced that the girl saw something, and, if she had, he would do his utmost to upset it. Shortly afterwards, an old lady died in the village and Morrison now had visions of something happening. He told his aged mother he was not going to the funeral, an unheard-of thing in a small community. His mother remonstrated with him and pointed out that there were only ten houses in the village, that the deceased was a relative, and that the whole village would be talking about his absence. There seemed to be no way out of it.

Unwillingly he decided to go, but deliberately chose a different partner to the one referred to by his maid. He chuckled to himself at the way he had upset the maid's vision, and what a tale for the ceilidh-house as to how he had again upset old beliefs!

The cortège left the house and wound its way slowly along the narrow road. As it came near the spot indicated by the maid, a man who was late for the funeral was seen approaching on the road. He met the cortège at the very spot pointed out by the maid. According to custom, he immediately took his turn at carrying, and, being the odd man, knocked all the others out of their partners—and Morrison found himself taking his turn with the newcomer as his partner, as foretold.

Another time Morrison was coming home from town after midnight with the local farmer's son. They had a horse and trap with them. The night was fine and the moon was full when they parted where the two roads branched off like a 'y'. Morrison had to go one way and the farmer's son with the trap the other. After walking about a hundred yards, Morrison looked across the meadow and saw the trap racing at a very fast pace down the road. He also noticed a light, like that of a cyclist ahead of the trap.

A few days elapsed before Morrison met the farmer again. He asked him if he had got home safely, and then said: 'By the way, what was that other light going down ahead of you?' 'Did you see that light?' asked the other in surprise. Morrison nodded that he did. 'Well,' continued Willie, 'I whipped up the horse as fast as he could go and I could not overtake that light one inch, and instead of turning in towards our own farm it continued on to my sister's. I lost it among the farm buildings. I woke everyone up and asked if any of the servants were out, but they told me everybody had gone to bed.' The following week Morrison's sister's husband was drowned in the harbour, and it was in that very same trap the body was brought home.

Barking dogs or crowing cocks at night, dreams of white horses or boats sailing on the land, were all omens of death. To see a person glowing as if covered with phosphorus was also a sure sign of death.

A very reliable friend was telling me she was coming out of the weekly meeting in the local mission-house when she saw the man in front of her all aglow with phosphorus. She began to brush down his jacket with her hand and asked where he had been sitting or whether he had been working with fish. He could see no phosphorus on himself and asked her if she was really seeing it. She assured him that she was. 'Ah well,' he replied, 'I am not long for this world.' He was drowned within a week.

Personally, I have never seen or heard anything appertaining to the supernatural, but I have had one or two interesting experiences. I was coming home from town one dark night. As I climbed Oliver's Brae I kicked a small parcel on the road. I could see sufficiently in the darkness to tell me it was cloth of some kind, and I concluded it was a linen towel.

Although it was late, my mother was still up and waiting for me. I showed her the parcel I had found. On unwrapping it, we got the shock of our lives to discover a long white garment, which turned out to be a shroud. But what was to be done with it? My mother would not hear of it being left in the house all night and asked me to put it in the barn until the morning. I hadn't minded carrying the thing as long as I didn't know what it was, but now that I did know, it was a different story. Having been brought up in an atmosphere of ghosts and spirit funerals, I didn't find the task much to my liking! However, I dared not show any signs of fear in the presence of my mother, so off I went. The thought of going into a dark barn at any time was bad enough, what with the heavy breathing of the cow and other eerie noises, but to face these conditions with a dead man's shroud under your arm was terrifying.

Fortunately, the barn was attached to the house and I had not far to go. One pane in the barn window was hinged to let the hens in and out, and by good luck it was open. There was only one thing to do—I threw the shroud in through the window and hurtled back to the house-door, whistling bravely as if nothing had happened!

We were aware, of course, that such a thing as a shroud would soon be missed, but then we had heard of no death in the nearby villages. Next morning we saw a gig approaching in the direction of the town. The driver and another man sat in front, and we knew by their dress and sad appearance that they were on some mission involving death. My mother stopped the gig and asked the men if they had lost something. They told us that they had taken the coffin home the night before and that the shroud, which was lying on the bottom of the gig, must have fallen out while they were climbing the brae. When the news got around that I had found a shroud on the road, I was asked all kinds of questions. 'Did you not feel anything strange about yourself? Did you not feel an uncanny weight on your hands or shoulders?' And so on. The questioners seemed disappointed when I told them that I felt nothing unusual, but they were convinced that something should have happened to me, to indicate that I was to handle a dead man's shroud.

Perhaps I may be allowed to digress for a moment while on the subject of coffins to tell the story of the village joiner in one of our remote villages who used to provide all the local coffins. Often they were made from crudely-sawn planks. The workshop was the local parliament, and particularly so when a coffin was being made. The conversation as a rule was about the deceased, but there was at times light, flippant talk as well.

On the occasion I am recalling, the joiner could not get the sides and the end to come together as well as he wished. There was quite a gap in the joint. 'Ach,' commented one of the spectators, 'isn't it good enough, Neil?' Neil adjusted his glasses on the point of his nose, looked at the man, and replied: 'Yes, good enough for you, perhaps, but it is not you who is going to pass the winter in it.'

Fairies were believed in by some; others were sceptical,

and today, few people believe in fairies at all. There was one woman in my native village who saw fairies daily and conversed with them. She knew them by name—Chonachag Popar, Labruchan, etc. When she was young she had been isolated to a small shieling on Cnoo Dubnaig owing to a fever. Like most other hills and knolls in Lewis, it was a fairy abode, and Mor came under the influence of the little people. They played all kinds of tricks on her. She had a pin-cushion behind the door, but it was of no avail.

I went into the house next door one day to pick up a friend who was going fishing with me. He was shaving at the time. Mor also came in and at once complained of these rascals who had followed her in. She got my friend to brandish his razor behind her head in order to scare them away. On another occasion, she got one of the villagers to fire his shotgun over her shoulder. Nevertheless, the 'rascals' would help her at times. When she went to the peat-bank for a creel of peats, they always helped her to get the creel on her back.

Mothers laid the tongs across the cradle when they went out in order to keep the little folk away. During my mother's time, one baby at least was carried off by the Daoine Sith or Men of Peace; a changeling was left in its place. I have known the man for many years. His mother had gone out to put some clothes on the bleaching-green and saw upon returning that her baby had disappeared and that a baby with a wizened old face had been left in its place. The elders or wise men of the village were consulted, and they advised that the changeling should be placed under an umbrella on the highway where three roads met. This was done, and the proper baby was restored to his mother.

24

THE FAIRY DOG'S TOOTH

The story that follows is about the well-known seer of old Holm, Alex Munro, my great-great-grandfather.

On the small beach at the end of Lower Sandwick near Stoneyfield, there is a sward of green grass on which people walk on their way to and from Holm Point. On one part can be seen a patch of earth resembling a coffin, where not a blade of grass grows. That is where a travelling salesman, who was murdered, is buried, and whose belongings were stolen from his pack. I am sure there are many in Sandwick today who do not know about it.

Since then, a light was often seen on the small beach. Older people used to say that something awful was going to happen on the shore—but it had already happened! The light was never seen again after Alasdair, son of Murdo, son of Finlay, had conversation with the light.

Alasdair was returning home from Stornoway to Old Holm. The evening was nice and mild, and there was nothing to be heard but the gentle lapping of the waves against the shingle.

Alasdair saw the light, blessed himself, and in the twinkling of an eye, an apparition was standing in front of him. Alasdair could do nothing but listen patiently. The ghost told him his story, that he was a travelling salesman who was murdered and buried on the shore, and that his spirit would have no peace until someone heard what had happened to him. Before parting, the ghost thanked Alasdair for listening, and as a gift, told him to lift a turf beside the Red Stone in the ditch, and there he would find the Fairy Dog's tooth, a tooth that would give him and his family power, as long as it stayed in their keeping. 'And,' said the ghost, 'as proof that this is true, before you go to bed tonight, there will be a mark on you that you will bear till the day you die.' Before Alasdair could wink, the ghost had vanished. He was frightened, but was not sure whether he really had seen a vision!

However, he arrived home in old Holm, close to the Beasts of Holm. As was common in those days, Alasdair lived in a black house, and the lintel stone was not placed high enough for someone as tall and sturdy as he was to walk under. Alasdair forgot to stoop and knocked his head against the lintel stone and got a gash above the eye—not a bad one—but a wart grew on his eyebrow which he carried till the day he died.

The following day, he took a walk up the croft to the Red Stone. He unearthed a sod as he was told and there was the tooth, the Fairy Dog's tooth. The news spread far and wide and they came from every district in the island to ask Alasdair's advice on all kinds of matters—if a cow or sheep was ailing, about crops, about friends who had gone to foreign lands and had never returned.

Now, many will think that this is another silly story. Let that be as it may, but I myself have handled the tooth. I was very young at the time, without knowledge or wisdom of what was happening. The tooth was the size of a fly or the back tooth of a horse, and I would say it had no resemblance to a dog's tooth—that is, if fairy dogs are like ordinary dogs. The tooth was in this family's keeping for many a year, and the last I heard about it was that the last person to own it died without son or daughter, and so the tooth fell into the hands of people who had no connection whatever with the family and took it to America.

That is how Alasdair got the tooth, and I am sure you would like to hear a story or two of what he did with it.

At the time of which I am speaking, there was a farm where the village of Aignish now is, and it was the Bailiff's daughter who was the mistress there. She was giving up the farm and she sent to Holm for Alasdair, since he was so well known in the district, to value the crops and animals. Alasdair did so, but evidently the valuation did not please the Bailiff's daughter. Alasdair's prices, in her opinion, were too low. So she invited Peter, one of the sons of a family from Garrabost, to value her animals and crops. Peter's valuation was higher and he got the job. As you may know, this did not please Alasdair from Holm, and so he started using the powers he had from the tooth against the man from Garrabost. And from all appearances, Alasdair was causing mischief, for nothing prospered for the Garrabost fellow. Crops were poor, cows had no milk, sheep fell into bogs, even the hens did not lay eggs as they used to.

Peter knew it was the Holm man who caused all the losses, and one day he took a leisurely walk up to Holm. There was a distance of only six miles between the two villages, and that was no distance in those days. He arrived in Holm, entered and was made welcome. He told them the reason for his visit and what was happening to him. He asked Alasdair for forgiveness, and to allow things to get back to normal.

'It was the croft I pronounced unproductive, not your animals,' said Alasdair, 'and I cannot reverse that. But I expect to go down to Portnaguran in a day or two to visit a friend who is ill. In passing, I shall walk on your croft and everything will be as before.' The man from Garrabost thanked him and returned home. Alasdair did as promised in a day or two, and that year seven calves were born for the Garrabost man!

The Fairy Dog's Tooth

There was another man from Steinish who was taking the peats home. He had a good team filling the cart out on the moor, and he himself was stacking the peats at home. There was a breeze and the peats were dry. As happened to many others working on peats on a dry breezy day, he got *smoor* (grit) in his eye. He thought nothing of it except that he kept rubbing it. Some people would say to him, 'You'll be all right in the morning. Sleep on it and it will go away'. But, although he did sleep, the eye was as annoying as ever. The upper eyelid would cover the lower one, and the eye would be moved from side to side, but nothing happened. Others told him to stand on top of the hill, facing the wind, and to blow his nose as hard as he could. He tried that, but the eye was as before. Hector's widow even put her tongue into it but, despite everything, all was as before. It was indeed annoying. At last they advised him to go to Holm, and if they weren't mistaken, Alasdair from Holm would relieve it. There was nothing for it but to do so.

He went across Sandwick Hill to Holm. He arrived at Alasdair's house and walked in. There was no knocker or lock on doors in those days. They recognised each other. He was welcomed and he sat on the bench by the fire. He told Alasdair what had happened and how he got the peat dross in his eye a week ago and though they tried and tried, the eye was still the same. Alasdair listened patiently. He said, 'Your eye is very sore, but I am sorry I can't do anything for you at the moment. But you go home, and if I am not mistaken, you will get relief before you arrive home. If you do, come back and tell me'.

The man set off to return to his home in Steinish, and when he was passing Sandwick Hill, he felt his eye was better. He winked a few times. Sure enough, whatever was in the eye had disappeared. As you have heard, he had promised Alasdair that he would return and tell him if he got relief. When he arrived at Holm and entered the house,

Alasdair was sitting at a small table beside the partition, a bowl full of water in front of him, and a thin wooden peg at hand. He raised his head when he saw the man from Steinish coming in.

'You have come back,' said Alasdair. 'Yes,' said the man. 'How is the eye?' said Alasdair. 'Whatever it was, it has gone. I am perfectly well now.' 'Come over here,' said Alasdair. 'Look at that,' pointing with the wooden peg to a piece of grit floating on the water in the bowl. 'That is what caused the damage.'

25

WAKES AND FUNERALS

Wakes are still common in the isles, and the body may be kept in the house for three days or more. The period is seldom over three days unless some relative has to travel a long distance to attend the funeral.

Highland people feel under an obligation to attend the funerals of relatives, and relationship in the isles means something more than simply brothers or sisters. Yes, it goes back into the third and fourth generation. The relatives gather from far and wide, and, if they have come a long distance, they remain with the bereaved until the burial has taken place.

Highland people are also very superstitious and they fear the supernatural. They are very psychic, too, and many villages had their own seers who heard strange noises and saw strange visions.

On death, the body lay for the first day or two at the side of the room on a board and trestles covered with white sheets down to the ground. In my young days the trestles were usually two barrels borrowed from neighbours and the board was an old barn-door. When draped with the white sheets, the barrels and door were not visible, and they served to all appearance just like the modern under-taker's trestles.

The crofters from whom the barrels and the barn-door were borrowed could tell beforehand that they were to be used for such a purpose, for from the barn they had heard strange, unusual, eerie sounds, and the lady from whom the sheets were borrowed had heard the cist open and shut during the night. Even the gravedigger could tell when a death was nigh, for the spades in his little shed rattled and moved about during the night.

The face of the corpse was covered over with a white cloth. Pictures and mirrors were taken down or covered or turned against the wall. The clock was stopped and people moved silently about the room; hardly a word was spoken and the silence was broken only by an occasional sigh.

Once I saw a saucer of coarse salt lying on the abdomen of the dead one. I was told it was to keep away evil spirits, while another said it was to absorb any offensive odours from the body.

There is no record, to my knowledge, of professional chanters or mourners being used in the Highlands and in the Isles as is done in Eastern lands, but I have seen on two occasions a female relative take on the chanting role.

On the first occasion, the woman was dressed in black and sat on a low stool near the fire. She rocked backwards and forwards, patting her hands on her knees, or sliding them back and forth on her legs. The chanting was in a monotone and just loud enough for all present to hear. The lament seemed to follow the *Oran Mor* type of Gaelic singing and was mournful, like Gaelic psalm-singing. The subject matter of the dirge was in praise of the deceased and was simply anything at all. One line I remember was: 'You bought a new suit and you never used it'. This was uttered in a monotone and rose to a crescendo.

On the other occasion, the woman sat on a heap of straw near the fire, which was in the middle of the floor. She also rocked backwards and forwards and appeared to be in great distress; pain and grief were apparent in every word. When she moved about the house she did not stand erect but proceeded slowly in a half-bent position. Only on these two occasions have I heard the chanting, although I attended on an average six or more wakes and funerals a year for about thirty years.

These customs probably linger still in the more remote corners of the isles, but in most parts wakes close at midnight. I remember the first house in my own village of Sandwick that broke away from the old tradition of all-night wakes. The breach was the main topic of discussion for a long time after and the perpetrators were referred to as barbarians and infidels. It was thought hard-hearted and un-Christianlike.

People gathered from all the surrounding villages for the wake. In the old black house both rooms were full of people and a service was conducted by a deacon or elder of the church to which the deceased belonged. Although people of all denominations attended the wake, only office-bearers of the dead person's church conducted the service. The services went on until midnight, when most of those present returned home. Those who intended sitting all night then begin to arrive. Some conversation was carried on during the night, but usually it was not sustained, as the whole atmosphere was subdued.

Tea and biscuits were served; very rarely have I seen any liquor, and emphatically no excess of liquor, being served, in spite of references published to the contrary by my friend and village neighbour Mr. Alasdair Alpin Macgregor. Never during my forty-eight years' residence in the isles have I seen one drop of liquor at any funeral.

The wake went on until the day of the funeral, usually about three days. On that day a morning service was held, as nearly all funerals in Lewis took place at 2 p.m. The previous day, two boys were sent round the village to tell the people that the funeral would be at two o'clock the next day. Boys of ten or twelve years of age loved this job, as it carried something of importance. The messengers were hardly necessary as everybody already knew that the mourner James or Norman had arrived the night before by the boat and that the funeral would be next day.

An hour or so before the hour of departure, people would gather from the various districts, dressed in their bowler or soft hats, black ties and long black coats. They lingered around the sheltered end of a peatstack or at the end of the house until the appointed hour.

Two pairs of chairs facing each other and about six feet apart were placed on the road and the bier was set down with its ends resting on the chairs. The bearer or the bier was always kept in an old quarry outside the village. Nobody would keep it at home as it was associated with the dead, and nobody wished to see it hopping around at midnight on its two lanky wooden legs! It was fetched the day before the funeral and lay against the back of the house.

The coffin was carried out by the chief mourners and laid on the bier feet first. Groups of half-hidden children peered at the proceedings. The men lined up in twos behind the bier. The weight was taken off the chairs, which were moved to one side. The procession moved on with a slow, steady, rhythmic step. The women gathered to the door and the weeping and lamentations slowly faded as the cortège moved on.

The bier was shaped like a wide ladder about twelve feet long with four handles or gripping places on each side. Thus eight people were carrying at one time. The rest of the mourners formed up in couples behind, and a funeral was usually attended by from fifty to a hundred people. The chief mourners held a tassel each, one at each end. They did not carry the bier.

The file of couples widened out at the rear of the bier and moved up on each side until the first two were abreast of the leading couple. After about twenty paces, the first two of the couples who had come up relieved the leaders at the bier, who then fell back to handle number two, while those at two in turn fell back to three, and those at three went to four. The couple at four fell out, one on each side, stood, back to the cortège, until the procession passed them, and then joined up at the rear. Sometimes, according to the distance from the cemetery, each couple would have quite a few carrying turns.

At the graveside the tassels were undone and the coffin was let slowly down by the chief mourners. All heads were now bared and a prayer was offered. Some Highland churches did not approve of graveside prayers. Could there be a more impressive moment for a prayer than beside an open grave?

Lewis graveyards, in the main, were on machair land, and I can visualise at the moment the cemetery at Eye in Point district, where many Macleod chiefs are buried. Here is the perfect place for interment—the sand over ten feet deep, the grave clean-cut. It was comforting to those who remained to know that the body of the loved one was in such a beautiful resting-place, undefiled by clay soil or even by a pebble. The graves for the most part lay east and west, with the head to the west, a custom probably coming down from very ancient times.

When the great trumpet sounds on the Day of Judgment, the faces of the dead will be to the east, towards the rising sun, where the glory of God will be manifest.